The Lord of Glory
CRUCIFIED!

The Lord of Glory
CRUCIFIED!

Meditations on the Death of Jesus Christ

Tim Shenton

Grace Publications Trust
175 Tower Bridge Road
London SE1 2AH
England
e-mail: AGBCSE@AOL.com

Joint Editors
J.P.Arthur M.A.
H.J.Appleby

First Published 1998
© Tim Shenton

ISBN 0 946462 52 6

Distributed by:
Evangelical Press
Faverdale North Industrial Estate
DARLINGTON
DL3 OPH
England

Printed by:
Creative Print & Design
Ebbw Vale
Wales

Cover design:
Evangelical Press

To my wife,
whose patience, understanding and
devotion to our children
have made this book possible.
She is prized more than rubies.

'Many women do noble things,
but you surpass them all.
Charm is deceptive, and beauty is fleeting;
but a woman who fears the
LORD is to be praised.'
(Proverbs 31:29-30).

Contents

The Death

The Burial

Foreword

As I look out the window of my study into our English garden, I see a variety of bushes, shrubs, plants and flowers. They all have a God-given beauty, but the roses are especially stunning, with their exquisite curves of pink or white. More often than not, when I look out into the garden it is with a hasty glance, and the beauty of the roses is missed. It is only when I single out the roses for special attention, and gaze upon them for several moments, that I am rewarded with the joy of God's creation.

If the whole Bible were a garden, then the four Gospel accounts of Christ's death would be blood-red roses. They deserve pre-eminence, though they represent just a part of the Holy Scriptures. The whole Old Testament leads up to the great event of Calvary. All the New Testament, once it has recorded what happened to Christ, goes on to explain the meaning of Calvary for a lost world. Christ's death is the theological and devotional centre of the Bible.

This volume of reflections on the death of Christ enables us to pause and concentrate on the details of Calvary. I suspect that many of us rarely do this, except possibly at Easter when the minister preaches a sermon on the cross. We read various portions of the Bible through the year, but do we single out the Calvary passages for special consideration? They deserve our attention far more than roses, and will yield up a reward for the earnest seeker. So pick up this book and read it alongside the Bible. Reflect on the issues carefully and mingle your meditation with prayer. It is from such prayerful reflections that the risen Lord is often pleased to revive his people.

Johnny Moore, July, 1998.

Introduction

'Never in the field of human conflict was so much owed by so many to so few.' These famous words of Sir Winston Churchill were in tribute to the young men of the Royal Air Force, who saved England in World War II. During the same war many United States servicemen lost their lives at the Battle of Bastogne. A monument there reads, 'Seldom has so much American blood been shed in the course of a single action. Oh, Lord, help us to remember!'

When we turn our attention to the cross upon which the Lord of glory died, it is well within the mark for us to say, 'Never in the history of the universe has mankind, and the whole of creation, owed so much to the God-Man who died on Calvary.' Since that day his death has been proclaimed to countless millions in every generation. It has been regarded by small and great alike as the 'most important, world transforming, and eternally significant event in the entire history of the world' (Krummacher). No one can ignore it. No one can refute its impact on the world. From the northern territories of Canada to the southernmost tip of Chile, from Siberia to South Africa, from the shores of mainland China to the coasts of the USA — all over the earth there are those who can testify to its transforming power. Because of it men, women and children are willing, not only to live for Christ, but to lay down their lives for him that his name might be glorified.

This book is the message of that cross and of the Saviour who died on it, a message that is 'foolishness to those who are perishing, but to us who are being saved it is the power of God' (1 Corinthians 1:18). 'Oh, Lord, help us to remember the cross!' is the prayer of the author.

The Crucifixion

As they were going out, they met a man from Cyrene, named Simon, and they forced him to carry the cross. (Matthew 27:32).

A certain man from Cyrene, Simon, the father of Alexander and Rufus, was passing by on his way in from the country, and they forced him to carry the cross. (Mark 15:21).

As they led him away, they seized Simon from Cyrene, who was on his way in from the country, and put the cross on him and made him carry it behind Jesus. (Luke 23:26).

Carrying his own cross, he went out to The Place of the Skull (which in Aramaic is called Golgotha). (John 19:17).

1.
Carrying the Cross

Our Lord's journey to Calvary was not the penultimate scene of a man whose purpose in life had failed, nor the tragic end of a soon-to-be-forgotten hero, but a journey, ordained in heaven, that culminated in the death of the Lamb of God, 'who takes away the sin of the world!' (John 1:29). It was a journey, painful in the extreme, it must be said, with its torment and grief, but glorious in the eternal fruit it ultimately secured. On that journey Christ bore an emblem of divine love. It was the cross. Today that cross is the Christians' symbol of conquest over sin and Satan. It is their stake of triumph over death and the world. It is the message of grace that will make the nations beat their swords into ploughshares and their spears into pruning hooks at the consummation of all things.

The Romans compelled criminals sentenced to death to carry their own crosses to the place of execution. It was a common enough practice, designed to humiliate the one condemned and to maximize the drama for those who watched. For many who bordered the path to Golgotha, the crucifixion of Jesus amounted to little more than a few hours of entertainment. It was an opportunity to see a 'false' Messiah paraded as an object of ridicule before his enemies, and a last chance to see the man who had stirred up Jerusalem with his teaching. They hoped he would perform another 'trick' that might extricate him from the hour of death. They had no idea that before them, struggling under the weight of the cross, was the Son of Man who, being in very nature God, 'humbled himself and became obedient to death 'even death on a cross!' (Philippians 2:8). Their minds were dull and their hearts hardened. In their view, Christ was an impostor, overcome by his own deceit and worthy of the cruelest condemnation.

Despite the scourging he had received, Jesus carried the whole cross (not just the crossbeam) for as long as he was physically able, probably for most of the way. That is why the apostle John makes no mention of Simon from Cyrene. Initially no one helped him. It was only when the soldiers forced Simon to intervene that the burden was removed. The cross itself, in view of the fact that an inscription was nailed above Jesus' head, was probably the so-called dagger-type or Latin cross depicted in many famous paintings. Ambrose, a renowned bishop of Milan (339-97), comments that the form of the cross was 'that of a sword with the point downward. Above is the hilt toward heaven, as if in the hand of God; below is the point toward earth, as if thrust through the head of the old serpent the devil.' At this point in Christ's passion many commentators refer to Genesis 22:6, where 'Abraham took the wood for the burnt offering and placed it on his son Isaac.' Interestingly, a Jewish writer speaks of Isaac carrying the wood 'as a man carries a cross upon his shoulders.'

When Jesus could no longer bear the weight of the cross, the soldiers 'seized Simon from Cyrene, who was on his way in from the country, and put the cross on him and made him carry it behind Jesus' (Luke 23:26). Simon was probably a Jew who had come to Jerusalem to celebrate the Passover. Some think he was a farmer who had come in 'from the country' after a hard day's work. He was a native of Cyrene, an ancient city in Cyrenaica in North Africa, which was located on a plateau about ten miles from the Mediterranean in what is now Libya. There was a Cyrenian synagogue in Jerusalem (Acts 6:9) and many Cyrenians were among the early Christians (Acts 11:20, 13:1). Mark mentions that Simon was 'the father of Alexander and Rufus' (15:21), who evidently were both well known among the Christians by the time Mark wrote his Gospel. In Romans 16:13 Paul tells his readers to 'greet Rufus, chosen in the Lord, and his mother (Simon's wife?), who has been a mother to me, too.' If the Rufus in Romans is Simon's son, it may be that Simon moved with his family to Rome soon after his encounter with Christ.

Initially, Christ bore the cross of sinners, but when its weight became too much to bear, a sinner bore the cross of Christ. What an inestimable honour to carry the Saviour's cross, though Simon at the time was not aware of the blessed privilege he was allowed to share. The soldiers forced him to carry the cross probably because he happened to be standing nearby. They had no other design than to use him to complete the task that had been assigned to them. They were ignorant of the fact that their random choice was governed by the providence of God and that they had carelessly picked a man whom God had chosen in Christ before the creation of the world; for many suppose that Simon, after he had witnessed our Saviour's death, believed on him. After he had laid down Christ's cross, he took up his own as a disciple and again 'carried it behind Jesus.'

As far as we know Jesus did not speak to Simon. Words were not necessary, for the dignity displayed by our dying Lord was a glorious testimony to his divinity, far more eloquent than a thousand sermons. Even the infidel Rousseau exclaimed, 'If Socrates lived and died like a sage, Jesus of Nazareth lived and died like a God!' Perhaps Jesus looked at Simon as he had looked at Peter after his denial, with tenderness and compassion, moving the fisherman to weep tears of repentance (Luke 22:61-62). If, as has been suggested, the events of that day changed Simon's life, then a day that started as any other, ended with one more soul enraptured with the glories of Christ. A most wretched and unwelcome task of carrying a criminal's cross, became a work that led to salvation by grace for the unworthy burden-bearer. A 'chance' meeting with a condemned man brought a guilty Cyrenian face to face with the Saviour of the world.

As was customary and according to law the execution took place outside the city of Jerusalem (Leviticus 24:14). He who had no sin became 'sin for us' (2 Corinthians 5:21), suffering 'outside the city gate to make the people holy through his own blood' (Hebrews 13:12). As our sin-bearer Christ was excluded from human society, so that we who have fallen short of God's glory could be included in the Israel of God. He was led out of the earthly Jerusalem that we might, through faith in him, be led into the heavenly Jerusalem. He was presented outside the camp as a sacrifice of atonement, so we could freely enter the Holy City and live in peace with God.

A large number of people followed him, including women who mourned and wailed for him. Jesus turned and said to them, 'Daughters of Jerusalem, do not weep for me; weep for yourselves and for your children. For the time will come when you will say, "Blessed are the barren women, the wombs that never bore and the breasts that never nursed!" Then

> *"they will say to the mountains, 'Fall on us!' and to the hills, 'Cover us!' "*

For if men do these things when the tree is green, what will happen when it is dry?' (Luke 23:27-31).

2.
The Daughters of Jerusalem

A large crowd gathered to watch the public execution. Many came out of curiosity to see the man who had performed so many miracles. Others were there to watch the sufferings of three condemned men. Some lined the way to witness a 'king' staggering to his death. But not all were opposed to him. God had reserved a small band of women who had not bowed to the demands of public pressure. These women must not be confused with those who had accompanied Jesus from Galilee (Luke 23:49), or with the women who had helped to support him and his disciples out of their own means (Luke 8:3); for they were 'daughters of Jerusalem' (Luke 23:28) who had probably resided in that city for some time. Luke recalls that, in a genuine outpouring of sympathy for an innocent man, they 'mourned and wailed' for Christ (Luke 23:27). They beat their breasts and, with heart-felt grief, laid 'one last flower for our Lord upon his path of thorns' (Van Oosterzee).

Such compassion was remarkable because, at least according to later Jewish tradition, it was against the law to show criminals any kind of sympathy on their way to death. It was also in direct contrast to the brutality of the soldiers (Matthew 27:27-31), the blasphemy of the religious leaders (Matthew 27:43), and the contempt of the majority who watched the procession of death wind its way slowly to Calvary (Matthew 27:39-40). It was certainly more courageous than the actions of Christ's disciples, who had already run for their lives. These men had no excuse for their unfaithfulness. They had witnessed firsthand the supernatural works of Jesus and listened to 'the words of eternal life' (John 6:68) from his lips. On the Mount of Transfiguration Peter, James and John 'were eye-witnesses of his majesty' (2 Peter 1:16) and heard the testimony of his Father: 'This is my Son, whom I love; with him I am well pleased' (Matthew 17:5). Peter had forthrightly confessed that Jesus was 'the Christ, the Son of the living God' (Matthew 16:16), and declared that 'even if I have to die with you, I will never disown you' (Matthew 26:35). And all the other disciples had said the same. Yet, when Jesus was arrested, 'all the disciples deserted him and fled' (Matthew 26:56).

Jesus had remained silent when questioned by Herod, but as soon as he heard the daughters of Jerusalem he turned to them and said, 'Do not weep for me; weep for yourselves and for your children' (Luke 23:28). This address may have been uttered as the cross was transferred to Simon, which would have given him a few moments to speak to his sympathisers before the soldiers drove him on. His message to them is surprising in that it is more a warning than a word of sympathy, more a promise of sorrow than of cheer, more a foretelling of desolation than an offer of consolation. It is a message that focuses on their need to repent, rather than on his own suffering.

Jesus knew that, although his hour of darkness was near, he was not going to be overcome by it. It was through the darkness of suffering and death that the Sun of Righteousness would rise to his greatest triumph. His future was secure. Eternal glory was awaiting him — it was but a moment away. But for these women the future was less certain. Unless they turned from their sin, blackest darkness would engulf them for ever. So as a matter of urgency Jesus told them not to weep for him but for themselves and for their children. He was calling them to weep over the sin that had driven him to the cross, and because of the judgment that would soon crush their city, which some of them would experience firsthand.

To weep for Christ as one would for any other afflicted individual reveals more about the sensitivity of human nature than the state of the heart before God. 'Melting affections are not infallible marks of grace, even when they proceed from a sense of Christ's sufferings' (Burkitt). If we are moved to tears at the injustice and cruelty that crushed Christ, an innocent man, but do not weep over the sins that caused his suffering, we may be near the kingdom of God but we cannot enter it. Tears of pity, even for Christ, cannot wash away sin. They may earn praise from our neighbours and enhance our reputation as men and women of compassion, but they do not prepare our souls for paradise.

'The right way to consider Christ's passion begins thus: that we, with our children, bewail ourselves and our sins' (Cramer). Instead of tears of compassion for Christ, it is more fitting that we weep over the sins that crucified Christ; instead of lamenting the cruelty of others, we must bewail the iniquity that plagues our own hearts. 'Blessed are those who mourn, for they will be comforted' (Matthew 5:4). Our wailing must not be for the sin-bearer, but over the sin that condemned him for our sakes. Our faith must not rest on the frailty of human pity but in the power of the cross and its message that saves all who repent and believe. It is the blood of Christ that 'cleanses our consciences from acts that lead to death, so that we may serve the living God' (Hebrews 9:14), not a sentimental heart.

In his reply to the daughters of Jerusalem Jesus predicted the catastrophic destruction of Jerusalem by the Romans. He foretold the anguished cry of its citizens: 'Blessed are the barren women, the wombs that never bore and the breasts that never nursed!' (Luke 23:29). Among Jewish women barrenness was a sign of reproach. Hence when Elizabeth became pregnant after many years of childlessness she praised God saying, 'In these days he has shown his favour and taken away my disgrace among the people' (Luke 1:25). During the conquest of Jerusalem such terrible times would engulf the city that barren women, previously thought of as living under the judgment of God, would be considered blessed by him. The children they never bore would escape the grief and slaughter that would sweep away other sons and daughters; and the childless couples, who may have earlier bemoaned their fruitlessness, would thank God for sparing them the pain of bereavement.

In AD 70 Titus, under the orders of his father Vespasian, marched against Jerusalem with a huge army. He besieged the city for about five months (from April to August), before razing it to the ground. During the siege the inhabitants of Jerusalem endured 'the most horrible sufferings from famine and pestilence that can be conceived. Women are reported to have actually eaten their own children for want of food' (Ryle). According to Josephus, a first century Jewish historian, the Romans slaughtered everyone they met 'and obstructed the lanes with their dead bodies. They made the whole city run down with blood to such a degree that the fire of many of the houses was quenched with these men's blood.' The aged and the infirm, as well as women and children, were brutally murdered, and prisoners were thrown to wild beasts. Those 'under seventeen years of age were sold for slaves' (ibid.). 97,000 were taken captive during the whole war and over a million perished in the siege. Most of the Jews who died were not citizens of Jerusalem, but had come to the city from other parts of the country to celebrate the feast of unleavened bread. Amid the festivities they suddenly found themselves shut in by the invading army. For many years after Jerusalem's destruction no Jew was permitted to inhabit or even to visit the city.

As Jesus approached Jerusalem, he looked over the city and wept. He knew that its citizens were going to reject him as their Messiah, and that caused him deep sorrow. He also knew that their enemies would soon 'dash you to the ground, you and the children within your walls. They will not leave one stone on another' (Luke 19:44). 'God's wrath,' says Rieger, 'is harder to bear than Christ's cross.' Indeed, to reject Christ's cross is to remain under God's wrath. If we say 'No' to the love and mercy that are held out to us at Calvary, all that is left for us is the damnation of the impenitent. It is senseless to deny the truth and to treat with contempt the blood of the new covenant, to trample the Son of God underfoot and to insult the Spirit of grace with our stubborn refusal to repent! 'How shall we escape if we ignore such a great salvation?' (Hebrews 2:3). To whom shall we flee in the day of wrath? Is there another atoning sacrifice for our sins? Is there a second Saviour in whom we can find forgiveness? Without Christ there is 'only a fearful expectation of judgment and of raging fire that will consume the enemies of God' (Hebrews 10:27).

The devastation and despair of those days will be so intense that both men and women will 'say to the mountains, "Fall on us!" and to the hills, "Cover us!" ' (Luke 23:30). This proverbial expression, with slight differences, occurs three times in Scripture. The first is found in Hosea 10:8, where God's judgment against Samaria is described. It is also quoted in Revelation 6:16, which pictures the final and most terrible day of judgment, when those under God's wrath will cry out to the mountains and rocks saying, 'Fall on us and hide us from the face of him who sits on the throne and from the wrath of the Lamb!' (cf Isaiah 2:10,19). In Luke Jesus predicts the utter hopelessness of all who will be caught up in the siege. Their distress will be far worse than they could have imagined and more agonising than anything they have experienced before. They will long to be crushed by falling rocks. Only in death will their anguish be stilled and their eyes closed to the slaughter. During the siege many Jews fled to caves or sheltered in subterranean passages and sewers under the city in an attempt to escape the enemy's wrath.

As Christians we do not need to pray to inanimate mountains and hills, pleading with them for protection. Nor do we flee to caverns to escape the enemy. God is our hiding place. He is our rock and fortress whose iron walls cannot be breached by our adversary. He is a strong defender, who upholds those who trust in him, and a mighty tower in which we find shelter from the storms of life. Though the narrow road that leads to life is often lined with perils, and though the devil stands by foaming out obscenities and threats that make us tremble, we need not fear, for the Lord has promised to rescue us from every evil attack and to bring us safely to his heavenly kingdom (2 Timothy 4:18). When we pass through the waters, they will not sweep over us; when we walk through the fire, we shall not be burned or set ablaze by the flames (Isaiah 43:2). Our Lord is an impenetrable shield around us. He is the conqueror who lifts up our heads.

Our Lord's final word to the daughters of Jerusalem is a further warning of the terrible fate that will overtake their city. 'For if men do these things when the tree is green, what will happen when it is dry?' (Luke 23:31). Jesus uses this well known proverb to contrast green or moist wood, which does not burn well and which is usually cast on the fire last, with dry or dead wood which is easily consumed and used only for burning. The meaning is that if the moist wood is burned, how much more will the dry wood be consumed by the flames; or if the green wood perishes, all wood must perish. The green wood represents Jesus, and the dry wood the unregenerate Jewish people. Therefore, if Jesus, God's only Son, has to suffer so acutely, what will happen to God's enemies? 'If the Romans practise such cruelties on me, who am a green tree and the very source of life, what will they do one day to your nation, which is like a barren, withered trunk, dead in trespasses and sins?' (Ryle).

Jesus endured the tortures of hell for a little while before he entered glory. The disobedient, if they do not repent, will be tormented day and night for ever and ever. Christians may be persecuted and experience all kinds of hardships, but the Lord in his time restores them and makes them strong, firm and steadfast (1 Peter 5:10). The unbeliever, unless he obeys the gospel, has no such hope of relief against the trials that buffet him. He has no promise of deliverance from the trap of the devil, who has taken him captive to do his will. So before we are tempted with the Psalmist to envy the wicked, saying: 'They have no struggles; their bodies are healthy and strong. They are free from the burdens common to man; they are not plagued by human ills' (Psalm 73:4-5), let us remember that though many saints at present groan in the fires of affliction, they will one day, along with all believers, be welcomed by God into the new Jerusalem, where there is 'no more death or mourning or crying or pain' (Revelation 21:4).

They came to a place called Golgotha (which means The Place of the Skull). There they offered him wine to drink, mixed with gall; but after tasting it, he refused to drink it. When they had crucified him, they divided up his clothes by casting lots. (Matthew 27:33-35).

They brought Jesus to the place called Golgotha (which means The Place of the Skull). Then they offered him wine mixed with myrrh, but he did not take it. And they crucified him. (Mark 15:22-24a).

Two other men, both criminals, were also led out with him to be executed. When they came to the place called The Skull, there they crucified him, along with the criminals — one on his right, the other on his left. (Luke 23:32-33).

Carrying his own cross, he went out to The Place of the Skull (which in Aramaic is called Golgotha). Here they crucified him, and with him two others — one on each side and Jesus in the middle. (John 19:17-18).

3.
The Crucifixion

Jesus was led out of the city with two other men, both criminals (Luke 23:32). Tradition names them as Titus and Dumachus and claims that Jesus had met them when in Egypt. Matthew and Mark both call them 'robbers'. Some think they were friends of Barabbas, who had been 'thrown into prison for an insurrection in the city and for murder' (Luke 23:19). Others regard them as just common thieves. Whoever they were and whatever their offence, the Holy One of God was numbered with them as if he were a partner in crime. To those who stood by, who knew nothing of Christ and his work of salvation, the three men could have been members of the same gang, deservedly trudging the road to death.

The procession at last reached 'The Place of the Skull (which in Aramaic is called Golgotha)' (John 19:17). The Greek word 'kranion' (cf the English 'cranium') and the Latin name 'Calvaria', from which we derive Calvary, both mean skull. Some scholars, thinking The Place of the Skull was either a common site for executions or a well-known burial ground, say it was so-called because of the exposed skulls and skeletons that lay there. This idea, though, is contrary to Jewish usage and to the ceremonial purity of the Old Testament. Others believe that the shape of the small mound on which the cross was fixed was skull-like; hence its name. A few still hold to the fanciful legend that mentions Golgotha as Adam's burial place!

It is not possible to pinpoint the exact location of Calvary. It may have been on the north side of Jerusalem, near the Damascus gate; or on the west side of the city, near the Jaffa gate. Early tradition supports the site now assigned to the

Church of the Holy Sepulchre. The apostle John says it was
'near the city' (John 19:20), and the writer to the Hebrews
positions it 'outside the city gate' (13:12). It was certainly near
a thoroughfare as both Matthew and Mark mention 'those who
passed by' (27:39; 15:29), and John, in his Gospel, points out that
many of the Jews read the sign that had been fastened to the
cross (19:20). Our search is complicated by the fact that the
boundary walls of Jerusalem have changed many times since
the crucifixion.

The exact location, however, is not as important as many
have thought. None of the Gospel writers pinpoint Calvary, or
mention the precise localities of Christ's birth and resurrection,
and wisely so. There are many people bound by superstition
who are ready to turn any religious site or relic into a shrine or
object of worship, just as Israel prostituted themselves by
worshipping Gideon's ephod (Judges 8:27), and later by burning
incense to the bronze snake that Moses had made (2 Kings
18:4). The German theologian John Lange says that the site of
the crucifixion is 'too holy to be desecrated by idolatrous
superstitions and monkish impostures and quarrels. The
apostles fixed their eyes of faith and love upon the great facts
themselves and upon the ever-living Christ in heaven.' It is not
the places that are to be venerated, but the Lord who visited
them. Christians do not pay homage to a mound of earth called
Calvary, but to the Saviour who died there.

Today, even in well-educated countries, there are many
who revere such objects as the holy grail (the cup said to have
been used by Jesus and his disciples at the Last Supper). They
believe it to be so magical that immortality, or at least good
health, is bestowed on anyone who drinks from it. For centuries
people have searched for it, made films and written books about
it, and even claimed it as their own, in the hope of procuring
some supernatural blessing.

Just before the soldiers nailed Jesus to the cross, they
'offered him wine to drink, mixed with gall' (Matthew 27:34) as
an act of mercy. According to Mark this wine was spiced with

'myrrh' (Mark 15:23), a bitter narcotic usually given to condemned criminals to deaden the pain of crucifixion. Some suppose it also accelerated their death. Johann Neander, a nineteenth century church historian, reports that 'in the days of the Christian martyrs, it sometimes happened that similar drinks were administered to the condemned on their way to execution by friends and brethren in the faith who accompanied them.' Matthew may have been thinking of Psalm 69:21a, which is here literally fulfilled.

At this point Jesus was undoubtedly very thirsty. He had so far endured the agony of Gethsemane, where 'his sweat was like drops of blood falling to the ground' (Luke 22:44); the brutal scourging, that would have sapped the strength of the strongest man; the sickening derision and violence of the soldiers; and the burden of the cross; but when he realised the wine contained a benumbing ingredient designed to stupefy, 'he refused to drink it' (Matthew 27:34).

How easy it would have been for Christ to drink to the dregs the paralysing draught offered to him! The soldiers would not have blamed him. Other condemned men satisfied their thirst at such times, and took advantage of this crude form of pain relief, so why not Jesus? The guiding principle of our Lord's life and death was to submit to his Father's will. 'Not what I will, but what you will'(Mark 14:36) was the rule of his conduct. Obedience to his Father was to be prized far above a temporary cessation of pain. He had been born to 'save his people from their sins' (Matthew 1:21) and to bear the whole 'punishment that brought us peace' (Isaiah 53:5), and no merciful intervention by Roman soldiers was going to distract him from it. Only by enduring the full agonies of the cross could he satisfy divine justice and secure eternal life for those whom God had given him out of the world.

There are only four words (three in the original) used by Mark to describe the most significant event in world history: 'And they crucified him' (15:24). The Son of God, who enjoyed the eternal and perfect blessedness of his Father's presence, and in whom 'all the fullness of the Deity lives in bodily form' (Colossians 2:9), was nailed to a wooden stake on which he descended to the abysmal depths of hell. He who is in very nature God 'humbled himself and became obedient to death — even death on a cross' (Philippians 2:8), so that we, who have sinned so grievously and fallen short of God's glory, could be 'justified by his blood' (Romans 5:9). Through the cross he cancelled the written code, with its regulations, that stood opposed to us and obtained eternal redemption for all who believe.

The Gospel writers do not emphasise the physical side of Christ's suffering, and rightly so, because Christ suffered far more than just physically. Nevertheless it is true to say that, because of the excruciating bodily pain, a crucified man as he hung on the cross 'died a thousand deaths'. Crucifixion has been adjudged the most 'extreme punishment, shame and torture that could be devised by the old world. Only the Inquisition, with its fiendish inventions, has been able to surpass this torturing death' (Lange).

Rome was not alone in crucifying criminals. Persia, Syria and Egypt all practised this form of punishment. It was not, however, part of the Jewish penal laws. Rome usually (but not always) reserved crucifixion for slaves, highway robbers, rebels, outlawed prisoners of war, and others who had committed heinous crimes. According to Josephus, when Jerusalem was taken by Titus, he crucified so many Jews around the city that space and room failed for crosses, and crosses could not be found in sufficient numbers for bodies. How ironic, that many of those who had urged the Romans to crucify Christ were themselves crucified by the Romans! It was not until Constantine the Great (c. 274-337) that crucifixion was abolished in the Roman Empire. Apparently, he acted 'from motives of humanity, and especially from respect to the cross of Christ as the sign of victory' (ibid.). What a transformation! Through the death of Christ the cross, for so long a symbol of reproach and condemnation, rose to be a mark of triumph and hope.

'According to Roman custom, the crucified were not taken down; they were allowed to die slowly, and in the case of young and strong men, this continued sometimes for three days. Their flesh was given to the birds or other wild animals. At times their sufferings were shortened by kindling a fire beneath, or allowing lions and bears to tear them to pieces. Jewish custom, however, did not permit that further atrocity, partly from a sense of humanity, partly from regard to symbolic purity. The bodies had to be taken down and buried. Hence the Romans used to break the legs (John 19:31-33), and with this "mercy stroke" the pain of the sufferer ended. If they were thought to be already dead, to make sure of death, the body was pierced by a lance (John 19:34)' (ibid.).

Wayne Grudem, a professor of theology, says that a crucified criminal 'was essentially forced to inflict upon himself a very slow death by suffocation. When his arms were outstretched and fastened by nails to the cross, he had to support most of the weight of his body with his arms. The chest cavity would be pulled upward and outward, making it difficult to exhale in order to draw a fresh breath; but when the victim's longing for oxygen became unbearable, he would have to push himself up with his feet. This gave more natural support to the weight of his body, releasing some of the weight from his arms, and enabling his chest cavity to contract more normally. By pushing himself upwards in this way the criminal could fend off suffocation. However, it was extremely painful, because it required putting the body's weight on the nails holding the feet, and bending the elbows and pulling upward on the nails driven through the wrists.' William Edwards, a doctor of medicine, adds that 'muscle cramps and partial paralysis of the outstretched and uplifted arms would add to the discomfort. As a result, each breath would become more agonising and tiring and lead eventually to asphyxia.'

Dr Richter, a pious German physician who died in 1711, has also described the crucifixion and its physical tortures. 'The cross pieces were nailed in their places on the upright posts, sometimes before, sometimes after, the posts themselves had been set up. Jesus and his fellow-sufferers, in either case, were stripped once more, as they had been before they were scourged. The centre cross was set apart for our Lord. He was laid on it either as it lay on the ground, or lifted and tied to it as it stood upright. His arms were stretched along the two cross beams, and his body rested on a projecting pin of rough wood misnamed a seat. The Romans then drove a huge nail through the palm (wrist?) of each hand into the wood. The legs were next bent up till the soles of the feet lay flat on the upright beam. Then they too were fastened, either separately, by two great iron nails, or over each other, by one (Psalm 22:16; Luke 24:39-40; John 20:25,27).

'The suffering in crucifixion, from which death at last resulted, rose partly from the constrained and fixed position of the body, and of the outstretched arms. This caused acute pain from every twitch or motion of the back, lacerated by the scourge, and of the hands and feet, pierced by the nails. These nails were driven through parts where many sensitive nerves and sinews come together. Some of these were mutilated, others violently crushed down. Inflammation of the wounds in both hands and feet speedily set in, and ere long rose also in other places, where the circulation was checked by the tension of the parts. Intolerable thirst and ever-increasing pain resulted.

'The blood, which could no longer reach the extremities, rose to the head, swelled the veins and arteries in it unnaturally, and caused the most agonising tortures in the brain. As it could no longer move freely from the lungs, the heart grew more and more oppressed, and all the veins were distended. Had the wounds bled freely, it would have been a great relief, but there was very little blood lost. The weight of the body itself, resting on the wooden pin of the upright beam; the burning heat of the sun scorching the veins; and the hot wind, which dried up the moisture of the body, made each moment more terrible than the one before. The numbness and stiffness of the more distant muscles brought on painful convulsions. This numbness, slowly extending, sometimes through two or three days, at last reached the vital parts, and released the sufferer by death.'

These physical sufferings, terrible though they were, only give us a faint glimpse of the horrors that our Lord endured on our behalf. It is probably true to say that only the damned in hell appreciate, at least in some small measure, what Jesus suffered on the cross, although even that comparison falls short; for they are receiving the due penalty for their own sins and only for their own sins, whereas Jesus, a Saviour who is set apart from sinners, is the atoning sacrifice for the sins of the whole world (1 John 2:2). The damned have never known peace with God, for their evil behaviour alienated them from him. Jesus, on the other hand, is essentially and eternally one with his Father, inseparable from divine love and glory, and perfect in holiness; yet on the cross we considered him 'stricken by God, smitten by him, and afflicted' (Isaiah 53:4).

When the executioners drove the nails into the flesh of the Son of God, little did they realise the significance of their actions. If only they could have looked down the passages of time, and seen countless millions in all generations the world over, worshipping the God-Man they were crucifying. How dumbfounded they would have been to behold guilty men and women climbing the hill of Calvary to find peace with God at the foot of the cross! How humbled to know that what they were doing with such arrogance was not the end of a fanatic's life, but a new beginning for sinners as insolent and as wretched as themselves! How awe-struck to see the filthy and vile made clean by the blood they were shedding! Oh that blood, spilt by the soldiers without a moment's thought! How many it has justified! How many it has redeemed from the curse of the law! How many it has purchased for God 'from every tribe and language and people and nation' (Revelation 5:9)!

There are no words eloquent enough to describe that scene of long ago, or to mark its ultimately glorious triumph. Every thought is a trifle in comparison with the reality. Only in eternity shall we begin to comprehend its matchless wonder and discover its unending fullness.

Above his head they placed the written charge against him: **THIS IS JESUS, THE KING OF THE JEWS.** *(Matthew 27:37).*

The written notice of the charge against him read: **THE KING OF THE JEWS.** *(Mark 15:26).*

There was a written notice above him, which read: **THIS IS THE KING OF THE JEWS.** *(Luke 23:38).*

Pilate had a notice prepared and fastened to the cross. It read: **JESUS OF NAZARETH, THE KING OF THE JEWS.** *Many of the Jews read this sign, for the place where Jesus was crucified was near the city, and the sign was written in Aramaic, Latin and Greek. The chief priests of the Jews protested to Pilate, 'Do not write "The King of the Jews," but that this man claimed to be king of the Jews.' Pilate answered, 'What I have written, I have written.' (John 19:19-22).*

4.
The Three Crosses

The soldiers 'crucified two robbers with him, one on his right and one on his left' (Mark 15:27). These two malefactors or revolutionaries may have been associates of Barabbas, who was released by Pilate instead of Jesus. The Roman Governor probably had them crucified with Christ in order to mock and insult the Jews, who had infuriated him by insisting that an innocent man should be condemned to death. It is as if he was saying to them, 'Here is your King, crucified with thieves! What do you think of him now?'

Although Pilate's actions were not directly aimed at humiliating Christ, it was still a gross injustice for Christ to be crucified between two robbers, as if he was one of them. What an indignity for him who was without sin to be declared in public no better than the vilest of men! How degrading for the Righteous One to be exposed openly to a shame and condemnation that was reserved for the villains of society!

Although it shocks us to see our Lord crucified between two criminals, it should not surprise us, for throughout his earthly life he was a 'friend of tax collectors and "sinners" ' (Matthew 11:19). He came from heaven without pomp or ceremony, not to take his place among the rich and privileged, but to 'release the oppressed' (Luke 4:18); not to be a physician to the healthy, but to heal the sick; not to give sight to those who thought they could see, but to shine the light of life into the eyes of the blind. His commission was to satisfy the hungry and bless the needy, to identify with the hopeless and befriend the lonely. His work was among the outcasts of society, the lepers and the prostitutes, whose plight burdened his soul. He sought out the widows and the fatherless, the helpless and the despondent, the demon-possessed and the suffering. He was more comfortable in the company of beggars than hypocritical Pharisees, more at ease with a repentant prostitute than a critical lawyer. If he had died of natural causes and been given a state funeral with all the trappings of wealth, it would have betrayed his life and counted against his ministry of preaching 'good news to the poor' (Luke 4:18). For him to be crucified between two thieves, may repulse us, but it heralds, gloriously, the true anointing that was on him.

For a clearer appreciation of these events, we must look beyond the malice of a Roman governor and the envy of an angry nation to the sovereign and almighty Lord, who uses the wicked dealings of both men and Satan to accomplish his purpose. First, Isaiah's prophecy that the Messiah would be 'numbered with the transgressors' (53:12) is literally fulfilled; and second, the penitent thief is welcomed into paradise, a trophy of grace that would not have been won if Christ had been crucified alone. 'So easy is it for God to bring good out of evil, and to make the malice of his enemies work round to his praise' (Ryle). The murderous intentions of Herod that forced Joseph and his family to flee to Egypt only served to fulfil the Old Testament prophecy: 'Out of Egypt I called my son' (Matthew 2:15). The persecution of the early church was the means employed by God to scatter the gospel throughout Judea and Samaria (Acts 8:1). At Calvary, Pilate's decision to crucify all three men together fulfilled an Old Testament prophecy, and brought Christ face to face with a thief who had been chosen by God before the creation of the world.

Augustine of Hippo says that 'three very different persons hung together on the three crosses of Golgotha. One was the Saviour of sinners; one was a sinner soon to be saved; one was a sinner about to be damned.' Each one in his own way proclaims the message of the gospel: The first says, 'Come to me, all you who are weary and burdened, and I will give you rest' (Matthew 11:28); the second, from personal experience, testifies, 'Everyone who calls on the name of the Lord will be saved' (Acts 2:21); and the third in agony cries, 'Unless you repent, you too will all perish' (Luke 13:3,5). On one of the crosses hung a penitent thief, who was ready to confess Christ as his king and to take hold of the eternal life to which he had been called. On another of the crosses hung a reprobate, whose life of sin had so hardened his heart and seared his conscience that with his dying breath he insulted the Saviour of the world, thus shutting himself out from the presence of the Lord on the day he comes. And on the middle cross hung the Son of God, who owns the only 'name under heaven by which we must be saved' (Acts 4:12).

Mark reports that it was 'the third hour when they crucified' Jesus (15:25), which is contradicted, supposedly, by John 19:14, where it says that the sentencing of Jesus took place 'about the sixth hour'. Some critics scoff at the idea that Jesus was sentenced by Pilate three hours after he had been crucified! This apparent inconsistency, however, is easily resolved. Mark is using the Jewish mode of reckoning, which is the third hour after sunrise; that is, about nine o'clock in the morning our time. John, on the other hand, is writing mainly to Gentiles in Ephesus and its surrounding area. He therefore uses the Roman civil daytime computation, as he does elsewhere in his gospel (1:39; 4:6,52). This means that sentencing took place about the sixth hour after midnight; that is, six o'clock in the morning our time. This would have allowed plenty of time for the various trials to be conducted, considering that Jesus was arrested the previous night and condemned by the Sanhedrin very early in the morning.

'The third hour was the dying hour of Judaism' (Lange) and the birth hour of Christianity. By his death Christ made the Old Testament ceremonial regulations unnecessary. From that time the high priest could dispense with offering sacrifices for the sins of the people, for Christ 'sacrificed for their sins once for all when he offered himself' (Hebrews 7:27). All the types and religious festivals, so meticulously observed by the faithful, could be left alone, for 'these are a shadow of the things that were to come; the reality, however, is found in Christ' (Colossians 2:17). Instead of men offering gifts on a bronze altar, the gift of eternal life, secured by Christ when he offered himself on the wooden altar of Calvary, could be received by faith. The days of shedding the blood of bulls and goats could be forgotten, for Christ 'entered the Most Holy Place once for all by his own blood, having obtained eternal redemption' (Hebrews 9:12).

Two robbers were crucified with him, one on his right and one on his left. (Matthew 27:38).

It was the third hour when they crucified him....They crucified two robbers with him, one on his right and one on his left. (Mark 15:25,27).

Two other men, both criminals, were also led out with him to be executed. When they came to the place called The Skull, there they crucified him, along with the criminals — one on his right, the other on his left. (Luke 23:32-33).

Here they crucified him, and with him two others — one on each side and Jesus in the middle. (John 19:18).

5.
This is Jesus of Nazareth, the King of the Jews

It was usual for a criminal on his way to crucifixion to have a tablet naming his crime hung around his neck. In accordance with this well-known ancient practice Pilate had 'a notice prepared and fastened to the cross. It read, **JESUS OF NAZARETH, THE KING OF THE JEWS'** (John 19:19). It is not known whether this superscription was initially placed around our Lord's neck. Some think the notice was written on a board covered with white gypsum with red or black lettering. Matthew calls it a formal 'written charge against him' (27:37; cf Mark 15:26), which was the only accusation his enemies could find to throw at him. It was so insulting to the Jewish people that none of them would have agreed with it. Both Matthew and Luke say it was placed 'above' his head (Luke 23:38).

The wording of the notice is slightly different in each of the four gospels. Mark, for instance, simply says **'THE KING OF THE JEWS'** (15:26); whereas Matthew writes, **'THIS IS JESUS, THE KING OF THE JEWS'** (27:37). But why the discrepancy? Perhaps the wording was in a different form in each of the three languages it was written: Mark translates the Latin, Luke the Greek, and Matthew and John the Aramaic. Perhaps the gospel writers only wrote down the gist of what they saw, the full title being: **'THIS IS JESUS OF NAZARETH, THE KING OF THE JEWS'**. If anything the difference proves the genuineness of the Gospel writers. These four men were not copyists, out to prove their authority by writing exactly the same thing. They were individuals, with their own thoughts, styles and agendas, who were 'carried along by the Holy Spirit' (2 Peter 1:21) to write, in their own distinctive manner, the inspired word of God.

In preparing the notice Pilate planned to insult publicly the Jews he despised by mocking their ridiculous demand for Christ to be crucified. He wanted to announce to the world that if the king of the Jews should be crucified, so should all Jews.

Pilate worded the notice in 'Aramaic, Latin and Greek' (John 19:20), so that as many people as possible could read and understand it. It was not his usual practice, but he wanted all the people who had come to Jerusalem to celebrate the Passover to be informed about the treachery of the chief priests and the whole Sanhedrin, and to carry that message home with them. Aramaic was the language spoken by the Jews in Palestine and used in their worship. It is the oldest language in the world and the language of the Old Testament. Latin was the official language of Rome, the ruling nation of the world. Greek, which was common throughout the Roman Empire, was the world language of commerce and culture, spoken mainly by the literary and educated. It was widely used because of the spread of Greek philosophy. Lange comments that 'the inscription, in this threefold form, must symbolise the preaching concerning the Crucified One in the three principal languages of the world: in the language of religion (Hebrew), of culture (Greek), and of the State (Latin, the language of law and government).'

The wrath of men serves to praise God, for unbeknown to Pilate, he had just written one of the greatest gospel sermons of all time and declared to the world an eternal truth. We could interpret the notice as saying: 'The one you behold is not like the malefactors on either side of him. He bears no resemblance to those who condemned him. He is as far removed from his executioners as anyone could be. He is a king, **THE** king, not just of Israel but of every nation under heaven. He is the **"KING OF KINGS AND LORD OF LORDS"** (Revelation 19:16). He is matchless in dignity and almighty in power. He rules a kingdom that outshines the sun, that outlasts the ages, and that surpasses in greatness all the kingdoms of this world. No one can usurp his authority or cast him from the throne. He was born a king, and even in death he reigns supreme. Come, all who pass by, and bow before your Majesty.'

With a few simple words, which he himself failed to comprehend, Pilate celebrated 'Christ as the Author of salvation, the Nazarene of God, and the King of a chosen people' (Calvin); announced the Son of Man's 'innocence, dignity and destination' (Van Doren); and honoured Christ as the eternal victor over Satan and the powers and authorities that submit to his rule. But Pilate did more than that. He sent out a challenge for people everywhere to acknowledge Jesus Christ as their own king and to pray with the penitent thief, 'Jesus, remember me when you come into your kingdom' (Luke 23:42).

It may have been Pilate who prepared the superscription, but it was God who moved Pilate's hand. Pilate may have been venting his frustration towards the Jews he hated, but God was writing an accolade for the Son he loved. Pilate had no idea of the significance of what he wrote, God though 'was guarding his Son's glory' even in death (Pink). At our Lord's baptism God said, 'You are my Son, whom I love; with you I am well pleased' (Luke 3:22; cf 9:35). On the Mount of Transfiguration he declared, 'This is my Son, whom I have chosen; listen to him' (Luke 9:35). At his death he set the divine seal of approval above Christ's head and announced to all generations the Messiahship, Kingship, and Lordship of his Son. The superscription was a divine title, written by the Father for the Son. It was a heavenly title, written from above to those below. It is an eternal title, never to lose its power or significance. How the devil must cringe before it and do all in his power to blot it out! But never! Never will the hand of wickedness erase it or the ages erode it. It stands for ever, unchangeable and irrefutable.

The chief priests of the Jews were angered by the notice, so they remonstrated with Pilate, 'Do not write "The King of the Jews," but that this man claimed to be king of the Jews' (John 19:21). The enemies of Christ always object when God's truth is declared. They tolerate and even encourage the most loathsome behaviour, such as the scourging and crucifying of an innocent man, but when the glory of Christ is preached they raise their voices in protest. The truth irks them, disturbs them, frightens them. To stop themselves from hearing it they cover their ears and yell at the top of their voices (Acts 7:57); or, as we have here, they endeavour to change it so it fits in with their godless fancies. So great is their hatred of the truth, that even 'the smallest spark of it is more than they are able to endure. Thus Satan always prompts his servants to endeavour to extinguish, or, at least, to choke, by their own darkness, the light of God, as soon as the feeblest ray of it appears' (Calvin). The chief priests only wanted to make a small alteration, add a word or two, but the meaning would have been perverted and the truth annulled.

If Satan's threats do not frighten us into denying the gospel, he tries to lull us into a false security that rests on our own righteousness and not on the righteousness that comes from God and is by faith in Christ. If his black designs do not pervert our faith in the truth, he pretends to be an angel of light in order to complicate that faith with human traditions and worldly philosophies. When his ends are not achieved by mob rule and violence, he engages the more subtle tactic of compromise. 'Just change a little here or there,' he suggests. 'No one will notice and it will be of little consequence.' Yet that 'little consequence' robs Christ of his glory and makes the truth unrecognisable. Thus the title above Christ's head, instead of heralding the majesty of our king, becomes an accusation against him, charging him with deliberate deception.

The chief priests felt rebuked and insulted by Pilate's notice. It charged them with crucifying their own king! They wanted Christ alone to shoulder the blame for 'impersonating' the Messiah, and to exonerate themselves and their nation of any guilt. They could not bear the thought that this 'blasphemer' (Matthew 26:65; Mark 14:64), who had humiliated them with parables and condemned them so openly, should be heralded a king, and their king at that! They had only just stopped shouting 'We have no king but Caesar' (John 19:15), yet before the world Pilate was declaring this 'criminal' to be the king of the Jews. The truth was too poignant, too disturbing; so they demanded a change.

'The heart is deceitful above all things and beyond cure. Who can understand it?' (Jeremiah 17:9). When the chief priests handed Jesus over to be crucified, they thought it was a deed worthy of the highest praise and an act that honoured God. They imagined themselves to be upholding the law, which they professed to follow so scrupulously. In their own eyes they were champions of its cause and the master interpreters; yet their traditions, based on human teachings, opposed the very truth they claimed to serve. They were the ministers of Satan, masquerading as servants of righteousness (2 Corinthians 11:14-15), and blinded by a religious zeal that rejected the true knowledge of God. How ironic, then, that in a way totally unbeknown to them, their actions fulfilled what God's 'power and will had decided beforehand should happen' (Acts 4:28).

We may make the most eloquent speeches about our religious devotion and persuade many of our obedience to God. We may even look the part adorned in sacred vestments and mitres. But unless our lives reflect the love of Christ, we are nothing more than a 'resounding gong or a clanging cymbal' (1 Corinthians 13:1). The Pharisees, with their wide phylacteries, flowing prayer shawls and long tassels, were on the outside a picture of religious perfection, but inside they were 'full of greed and self-indulgence' (Matthew 23:25). It is not what we say or how we look that counts, but what we do. Jesus said, 'By their fruit you will recognise them' (Matthew 7:16). If our declaration of faith in Christ is not supported by a life of love and self-denial, then we are unworthy of our profession. We may adhere to orthodox doctrines and in public perform a variety of religious duties, but if we do not bear good fruit before God, we shall be 'cut down and thrown into the fire' (Matthew 7:19).

Pilate's response to the chief priests was abrupt and uncompromising: 'What I have written, I have written' (John 19:22). It may be that, after his wife's dream and warning (Matthew 27:19) and because of the accusations of his own conscience, Pilate was not prepared to condemn 'that innocent man' further. 'It is no uncommon thing to see a wicked man, when he has given way to the devil and trampled on his conscience in one direction, trying to make up for it by being firm in another' (Ryle). He had already handed Jesus over to be flogged and then crucified in order to satisfy the demands of the rabble. He was certainly not going to do anything else for them. Besides, why should he submit to the protestations of a people he despised? It was no concern of his if the Jews were publicly ridiculed for crucifying their own king. That was their own fault!

So Pilate, conscious of his own injustice and the innocence of Jesus, and rankled by his enemies' victory, refused to acknowledge Christ as guilty. He stood firm, like a rock, and in the words of the notice accused the Jews of disloyalty both to Caesar and to their own king. 'Most wonderful, that he who before was so vacillating, is now fixed as a pillar of brass' (Flavel).

The Roman governor was held by a divine hand that supported him to fulfil heaven's decree. It imparted to him a resolution not to bend, and a steadfastness that would not waver when pressed. God inspired him to write the notice, just as he had inspired Caiaphas to prophesy 'that Jesus would die for the Jewish nation' (John 11:49-50), and he emboldened him not to change it. 'Oh ineffable working of divine power, even in the hearts of ignorant men! Did not some hidden voice sound from within, and, if we may say so, with clamorous silence, say to Pilate, "Alter not the inscription of the title?"' (Augustine). Calvin rightly states that 'Pilate's firmness must be ascribed to the providence of God' (Calvin), whose word stands for ever, unshakeable and true (1 Peter 1:25). 'Not the smallest letter, not the least stroke of a pen' will by any means disappear from it (Matthew 5:18).

Not only that, but God would not permit the glory of his Son to be overshadowed or dimmed. Christ is the 'radiance of God's glory and the exact representation of his being' (Hebrews 1:3). In him are hidden all the treasures of divine wisdom and knowledge (Colossians 2:3), and in his face 'the light of the knowledge of the glory of God' shines (2 Corinthians 4:6). No cloud of compromise could therefore hide his splendour. No rubber of protest could erase his dignity. He is the King of kings before whom every knee should bow in heaven and on earth and under the earth, and to whom every tongue must sing its praise. The chief priests voiced their disapproval, but they could not suppress the truth of God — the truth every creature either lives by or dies without.

A heathen governor, hardened by sin and indifferent to the claims of Christ, refused to compromise the truth. How much more then should we, who are participators of the divine nature and indwelt by the Holy Spirit, uphold the gospel's demands and defend the Lordship of Christ. How easy it is to remain silent when the moment invites a response for Christ! How easy to water down the truth so as not to offend! When taken by surprise, if we do not watch and pray, we may quickly shame ourselves and the Saviour we love by echoing Peter's denial: 'I don't know him' (Luke 22:57). When men spit out their blasphemies, though it is natural at such times to skulk away and hide, we must 'be strong in the Lord and in his mighty power' (Ephesians 6:10). Let us take up 'the shield of faith, with which we can extinguish all the flaming arrows of the evil one' (Ephesians 6:16). Our responsibility is to stand firm despite the dangers, and to give ourselves wholly to the work of the Lord (1 Corinthians 15:58), even when the world is furious.

So let nothing move us from the truth that is in our hearts and which we should feel compelled to proclaim. Let us, with gentleness and faithfulness, confess Christ, not just in the privacy of our homes or in the security of a church building, but openly before the men and women of the world. Let us worship him, obey him, love him, without diluting his word or softening his commands, and so shine like stars in a crooked and depraved generation. It may just be that our testimony, however feeble, is the means that God employs to open the eyes of a man like the crucified thief, who embraced as his Lord '**THE KING OF THE JEWS**'.

Jesus said, 'Father, forgive them, for they do not know what they are doing.' (Luke 23:34).

6.
'Father, Forgive Them'

Has there ever been a more gracious expression of divine love for the unworthy, or a more earnest plea for the salvation of sinners than Christ's intercession from the cross? Has there ever been an utterance so heavenly in tone, or so profound in its revelation of God! What beauty and eloquence! What divinity! What an 'unequivocal proof of the majesty of our Lord in the midst of his deepest humiliation. It is the worthy conclusion of his earthly, and the striking symbol of his heavenly, life!' (Van Oosterzee). Surely, even to the natural unenlightened mind, Christ's petition discloses something of the glory of God's nature.

The first three words that Jesus spoke from the cross are all concerning persons near to him: his enemies, including the soldiers and Jewish leaders (Luke 23:34); the penitent robber (Luke 23:43); his mother Mary and John, the disciple whom he loved (John 19:26-27). And all three words exhibit the self-forgetfulness of Christ. 'Father, forgive them...,' the first of the words, was probably uttered by Jesus during the act of crucifixion, that is, as the soldiers hammered in the nails, and is an earnest request that his Father, who is ever ready to show mercy, would blot out the transgressions of those who tormented and mocked him. 'As soon as the blood of the great sacrifice began to flow, the great high priest began to intercede' for sinners (Ryle). During his earthly life Jesus had taught his disciples to 'love your enemies and pray for those who

persecute you that you may be sons of your Father in heaven'
(Matthew 5:44-45). In death he put into practice what he had
preached to others and thereby proved his divine Sonship.

It is so easy when we are wronged to slander our neighbour
and, because we feel unfairly treated, to attack in return. If
upset, our natural reaction is to strike back. We think it is our
right to do to them as they have done to us. In our haste to repay
an injury, we forget to 'overcome evil with good' (Romans
12:21) and to 'bless those who persecute us' (Romans 12:14).
When Stephen, 'a man full of God's grace and power' (Acts
6:8), was being stoned to death, he fell on his knees and, like
Christ, prayed for his executioners: 'Lord, do not hold this sin
against them' (Acts 7:60). He repaid evil with blessing and
hatred with love, and at the same time set the whole of
Christendom an example to follow.

Christ's prayer for his enemies firstly fulfilled Isaiah's
prophecy that the Messiah would make 'intercession for the
transgressors' (53:12). Secondly, it unveiled to both Jews and
Gentiles the eternal purpose of God: 'For God so loved the
world that he gave his one and only Son, that whoever believes
in him shall not perish but have eternal life. For God did not send
his Son into the world to condemn the world, but to save the
world through him.' (John 3:16-17). And thirdly, it so beautifully
unveiled the true nature of God, as he who is without sin, under
the most severe suffering, 'pleaded with God the Father for the
salvation of those by whom he was most cruelly tormented'
(Calvin).

There are two important questions that arise from Christ's
intercession. The first is: For whom did he pray? Some are of
the opinion that it was only for the soldiers who nailed him to the
cross, and who afterwards divided his clothes among
themselves. This view, however, is too restrictive. The soldiers
may have been central figures in the crucifixion, but they were
by no means the only enemies of Christ who 'did not know what
they were doing'. God's love for the world (John 3:16) and

Christ's own teaching about praying for persecutors (Matthew 5:44), compel us to believe that he interceded for all his tormentors, both Jews and Gentiles. This of course includes the Roman soldiers, but it also covers the men of Israel who 'acted in ignorance' (Acts 3:17), as well as their leaders, those members of the Sanhedrin who had deliberately plotted Christ's downfall. William Hendriksen, an outstanding New Testament scholar, argues that the Sanhedrin, 'though they must have known that what they were doing was wicked, did not comprehend the extent of that wickedness.' Paul, in his letter to the Corinthians, says that if the rulers of this age had understood God's wisdom, 'they would not have crucified the Lord of glory' (1 Corinthians 2:8). In other words, the rulers of the Jews knew that it was wrong to crucify Christ, but they did not know that Christ was the 'Lord of glory.'

The second question is: Was Christ's prayer answered? In the sense that Jerusalem was spared by the Romans for another forty years, the answer is yes. During this time the message of the cross was faithfully preached and many thousands were saved. On the day of Pentecost, after Peter's sermon about the death and resurrection of Christ, 'three thousand were added to their number' (Acts 2:41). Many of these new converts had no doubt urged Pilate to 'Crucify him!' and then ridiculed Jesus as he hung on the cross. After their conversion they devoted themselves to the apostles' teaching and 'the Lord added to their number daily those who were being saved' (Acts 2:47). Soon afterwards 'the number of men grew to about five thousand' (Acts 4:4). A large number of priests, the majority of whom had previously consented to Christ's death, also 'became obedient to the faith' (Acts 6:7). Later on in Acts we read that the Gentiles were granted 'repentance unto life' (11:18), and that the gospel spread into many foreign lands. In all this it must not be forgotten that one of the robbers, who had earlier 'heaped insults on him' (Matthew 27:44), asked to be remembered by Christ when he came into his kingdom

(Luke 23:42), perhaps as a direct result of hearing Christ's prayer for his enemies; and that the centurion and those with him who were guarding Jesus, after they had seen all that had happened, exclaimed: 'Surely he was the Son of God' (Matthew 27:54).

This delay in the outpouring of God's wrath, however, is no reason for the careless to postpone repentance, thinking that divine retribution has passed them by, for although Jerusalem was not destroyed immediately, it was destroyed. There are many who scoff at the thought of God's judgement, saying, 'Where is this "coming" he promised? Ever since our fathers died, everything goes on as it has since the beginning of creation' (2 Peter 3:4). They convince themselves that because God has not judged immediately, he will not judge at all. They forget that the old world, although it was given 120 years to repent, was eventually 'deluged and destroyed' (2 Peter 3:6); and that in a later century Jerusalem, after repeated warnings, was razed to the ground by the Babylonians in accordance with God's word.

These scoffers, if they admit to divine judgement, imagine themselves to be outside its jurisdiction. All that is necessary, they say, is to 'take life easy; eat, drink and be merry' (Luke 12:19). But does not God say, 'My Spirit will not contend with man for ever' (Genesis 6:3)? Are not 'the present heavens and earth reserved for fire, being kept for the day of judgement and destruction of ungodly men' (2 Peter 3:7)? How then do the impenitent expect to escape his wrath? It is true that 'the Lord is slow to anger', but he is also 'great in power; he will not leave the guilty unpunished' (Nahum 1:3). God is unquestionably patient 'not wanting anyone to perish, but everyone to come to repentance' (2 Peter 3:9), but if we refuse to obey his word and turn from our sin, despising his forbearance, then he will act against us, suddenly and with irresistible force.

Until that day of wrath comes, though, there is hope for the wicked, especially when Christians follow Christ's example and pray for their enemies. Are you like Christ's executioners, hardened in sin and indifferent to the suffering of God's Son? Watch out! For in the hands of God the prayers of the saints are like hammers that break stony hearts and as arrows that pierce the soul. In answer to them you may find yourself declaring with the centurion, 'Surely this was a righteous man' (Luke 23:47). Are you imitating the rulers, who actively opposed the purpose of God and who were so busy sneering that they never heard Christ's petition? Wait! When those around start to plead your cause before the throne of heaven, it may be that, through the silent working of God, your words of derision turn to songs of adulation, and your opposition to Christ becomes unashamed support for him.

Perhaps the burden of guilt has overwhelmed you, crushing any hope you had of salvation. Perhaps cultural prejudices have deceived you so you think the cross is void of meaning. Maybe you are engrossed in a life of crime to such an extent that your Christian neighbours only pray for your soul with feeble faith. Maybe you have spent days indulging in every kind of impurity, thus searing your conscience as with a hot iron, and believing that even if the whole world prayed for you, God would not listen to their pleadings. Not so! For when the righteous pray in faith, God's ears are attentive to their cry (1 Peter 3:12) and mountains are moved. It may be impossible for you to force your way into the kingdom of God, or to earn a pass by merit, but when your Christian friend intercedes on your behalf, he is, as it were, helping to bridge the gap between heaven and earth and taking hold of the living God, with whom nothing is impossible (Luke 1:37).

If as Christians we know of those who, naturally speaking, are beyond redemption, let us not stop praying for them. Remember how God transformed Paul, 'once a blasphemer and a persecutor and a violent man' (1 Timothy 1:13), into a servant of heaven, who spent his days 'preaching the faith he once tried to destroy' (Galatians 1:23). He is therefore quite able to turn our ungodly neighbours into 'instruments for noble purposes, made holy, useful to the Master and prepared to do any good work' (2 Timothy 2:21). Were we not at one time the same as those who now challenge our faith in God's redeeming power? So let us keep on praying to him 'who is able to do immeasurably more than all we ask or imagine' (Ephesians 3:20).

And if at times it is hard to pray, do not be discouraged or give up. God is just as able to answer a prayer that has struggled from our hearts battered by doubts as one that has flowed without hindrance in the fulness of faith. The prayers of the night are heard by God as easily as the prayers of the day. It is not whether the arrows of supplication are fired in strength or in weakness that matters to our omnipotent Lord, but whether they are fired at all. So let us keep on praying for the godless, however forlorn their case may appear to us, for nothing is too hard for God (Jeremiah 32:17).

When they had crucified him, they divided up his clothes by casting lots. And sitting down, they kept watch over him there. (Matthew 27:35-36).

Dividing up his clothes, they cast lots to see what each would get. (Mark 15:24b).

And they divided up his clothes by casting lots ... The soldiers also came up and mocked him. They offered him wine vinegar and said, 'If you are the king of the Jews, save yourself.' (Luke 23:34b, 36-37).

When the soldiers crucified Jesus, they took his clothes, divided them into four shares, one for each of them, with the undergarment remaining. This garment was seamless, woven in one piece from top to bottom. 'Let's not tear it,' they said to one another. 'Let's decide by lot who will get it.'
This happened that the Scripture might be fulfilled which said, 'They divided my garments among them and cast lots for my clothing.'
So this is what the soldiers did. (John 19:23-24).

7.
The Soldiers

The order of events now under consideration was probably as follows: our Lord was stripped of his clothes, which were put to one side; the soldiers nailed his hands and feet to the cross as it lay on the ground, fastened the notice above his head, and then fixed the cross into its upright position; then, returning to the clothes they had discarded, they cast lots for them.

The Roman custom of the time allowed executioners to divide the clothes of a condemned man among themselves. So 'when the soldiers crucified Jesus, they took his clothes, divided them into four shares, one for each of them, with the undergarment remaining. This garment was seamless, woven in one piece from top to bottom' (John 19:23). As the clothes were of unequal value they decided how to share them by casting lots (Matthew 27:35), perhaps by throwing dice. The first four pieces of clothing — the headdress, sandals, outer robe and sash — were divided into four shares, one for each of the four soldiers (cf Acts 12:4). The undergarment that remained was a seamless tunic, which was 'worn next to the skin like a shirt, mostly without sleeves, fastened round the neck with a clasp, and usually reaching to the knees' (Schaff).

In Roman times the clothes of the dead were often burned, sold or given away. It was an act that stressed the finality of the death. Luther remarks that 'the soldiers did not divide the clothes from need, or for gain, but in the way of jest. Their purpose was to enjoy a laugh, and to show that it was now all over with this Christ, that he was utterly ruined, destroyed and never more to be heard of.' The soldiers imagined that Christ would soon be like all the others they had crucified — an abandoned and forgotten corpse, left to rot in a tomb or grave. If they had heard of Christ's resurrection claim, they certainly did not believe it.

The soldiers realised that it was senseless to tear Christ's seamless garment as then each of them would receive only a small part, which would be of no use or value. So they said to one another, "'Let's not tear it. Let's decide by lot who will get it." This happened that the Scripture might be fulfilled which said, "They divided my garments among them and cast lots for my clothing." So this is what the soldiers did' (John 19:24).

The Old Testament Scripture that is here fulfilled had been uttered by David a thousand years before (Psalm 22:18). Hendriksen says that the woes described in that Psalm have 'reference directly to Christ, and were fulfilled in him alone, though in the life of David they were dimly foreshadowed.' Calmet comments that 'by occasion of his own griefs and sorrows David describes the passion, death, burial and resurrection of the Messiah, the calling of the Gentiles, and the rise of the church. This is his first and chief object. If he does now and then speak of himself, he does so only as he is a figure of Jesus Christ. In many places though David himself is entirely lost sight of.'

The soldiers remained oblivious to the fact that their actions were declaring to a watching world the eternal truth that 'the Scriptures cannot be broken' (John 10:35). They knew nothing of the Psalms and yet they fulfilled them. David was a nobody to them, yet they carried out his prophecy. They were mindless and godless, blinded by their own sin, and wholly unaware that they were the supporting cast in the work of the cross, whereby 'God was reconciling the world to himself in Christ, not counting men's sins against them' (2 Corinthians 5:19). Just as Moses lifted up the snake in the desert, so these legionnaires, who cared nothing for Christ or his word, lifted up the Son of Man, 'that everyone who believes may have eternal life in him' (John

3:14-15; cf 12:32). Now, centuries later, they are remembered, not for their obedience to the word of God, but for their degrading and insulting behaviour towards Christ and their unwitting fulfilment of the Scriptures.

Despite their shocking behaviour, all who love the Saviour they so cruelly treated, must feel some sympathy for them. For although they came face to face with Christ, 'a light for revelation to the Gentiles' (Luke 2:32), they did not see him through the eyes of faith. As a result they wandered from the cross with only the second-hand clothes they had cast lots for.

Is it not the same with many churchgoers today? The glories of Christ and his sacrifice are opened before them, and the eternal realities of heaven and hell resound in their ears. Their hearts are moved by the preacher's descriptions of the selfless love of God — but to no avail. For as soon as they step into the street their minds return to the things of this world and Christ is left behind. The seed falls along the path and the evil one, who waits outside the chapel gates, snatches away with wicked delight what was sown in their hearts. Maybe what the preacher says frightens them. His message is too powerful, too glorious, too life changing for them to embrace. The majesty and awesomeness of God that he unfolds is beyond their comprehension and that disturbs them. They feel they must loose themselves from the grip of what they have heard. So they march out into the open and almost audibly echo the words of the people of the Gadarenes, who pleaded with Christ to leave their region.

Stay and hear the message of the cross! It is the power of God to those who are being saved (1 Corinthians 1:18). Do not turn away from the crucified Lord. Look to him who was stripped of dignity so we could be clothed with honour. Turn to him who descended to the deepest depths of suffering in order to raise us to the highest heights of blessing. The first Adam sinned and the Lord God clothed him in garments of skin; the second Adam, who is without sin, was uncovered so we could be adorned with the garments of splendour. He was robbed of his earthly raiment, so we could be 'clothed with our heavenly dwelling' (2 Corinthians 5:2-4). He was shamed in weakness, so we could be 'clothed with power from on high' (Luke 24:49). He perished in nakedness, before the mocking gaze of his enemies, so we could be 'clothed with the imperishable' (1 Corinthians 15:54) and appear in glory before his Father's throne. He was unveiled as the sin-bearer of the world, so that in him 'we might become the righteousness of God' (2 Corinthians 5:21). Through the torments of hell he purchased for us the white robes of heaven (Revelation 6:11). What humiliation for our exaltation!

Our Lord Jesus Christ was immeasurably wealthy 'in the actual and constant possession of all divine perfections and prerogatives' (Hodge). Yet for our sakes he became poor, so that through his poverty we might become rich (2 Corinthians 8:9). He died that we might live. Such self-sacrifice is the proper test of love. 'This is how we know what love is: Jesus Christ laid down his life for us' (1 John 3:16). Therefore, as imitators of Christ, we ought to lay down our lives for our brothers. We ought to love, not 'with words or tongue, but with actions and in truth' (1 John 3:18). We ought to be like the good Samaritan, who gave his time and money to help a stranger. Let us use the riches that are ours in Christ to comfort the broken-hearted, to feed the poor, to help the needy, and to set the oppressed free. Then we shall be promoters of God's glory and useful in extending his kingdom.

Poor wretched soldiers! After the cruel exertions of that never-to-be-forgotten day, they sat down and kept watch over Christ (Matthew 27:36) to ensure that no one tried to take him down from the cross. During their long vigil they made no effort to dissuade passers-by from hurling insults at their innocent victim. No word in defence of Christ was spoken by them to silence the taunting Jewish rulers. Nothing was said to curtail the abuse that streamed from the robbers' lips. In fact, the soldiers soon joined the ranks of the scoffers 'and mocked him' themselves. 'They offered him wine vinegar and said, "If you are the King of the Jews, save yourself" ' (Luke 23:36-37). They ridiculed the idea of a king dying like an impotent criminal, treating Christ as a usurper, who had no subjects to submit to his authority, no kingdom to rule and no army to lead into battle. In their eyes, crucifixion was not enough for this 'pretender', so they humiliated him beyond compare and wounded him with the heavenly truths he had openly professed.

The world in its wisdom fails to grasp why the 'Lord of glory' (1 Corinthians 2:8) had to die in weakness and shame or why it was necessary for the Christ, 'who is the image of God' (2 Corinthians 4:4), to be afflicted in such a degrading manner. It cannot understand a Saviour who would not save himself, a Son of God who was forsaken by his heavenly Father, a high priest who wanted to destroy the temple. It is bemused by these apparent contradictions. With all its 'wisdom' it is blind to the glory of a high priest who fulfilled the shadows and brought in the reality; of a Son who was obedient to his Father, even to death on a cross; of a Saviour who offered himself for the sins of the world (Heubner). But to all who through God's grace have come to know the truth, to those whom God has called and who see with the eye of faith, both Jews and Greeks, 'Christ is the power of God and the wisdom of God' (1 Corinthians 1:24).

For six hours these rude legionnaires gazed 'on what has touched the world ever since, and what angels desired to look into, and saw nothing but a dying Jew' (Maclaren). At the end of that time, after witnessing our Lord suffer unto death and many of the extraordinary events that surrounded his demise, they exclaimed, 'Surely he was the Son of God!' (Matthew 27:54). The mockers, at least for the moment, became worshippers. Those who had cursed Christ now confessed him. It is improbable that the soldiers' declaration stemmed from personal salvation. It is more likely that, being so impressed with all that had happened, they reacted to it by making an impromptu statement of faith. Even hardened executioners, when confronted with the power and glory of Christ's death, are compelled to acknowledge his majesty.

It is equally interesting and by no means accidental that these soldiers were stationed at the foot of the cross to guarantee Christ's death. Crucifixion was a form of capital punishment, a lethal stake that ended life amidst unbearable agonies. Part of the soldiers' duty was to secure beyond doubt the death of their charge. If Jesus had been allowed to die in private, without this assurance and without witnesses, how many of God's enemies would claim that he had only fainted before being rescued by his friends, and that no sacrifice for sins had been made? As it is, the testimony and deadly expertise of four professional executioners supplies ample evidence that the Good Shepherd did indeed lay down his life for the sheep.

Praise be to God that Christ came and died to save sinners, the worst of whom lies within the range of the redeeming power of the cross. Thank God that there is always room for one more at the foot of Calvary's tree and that Christ's blood can make the vilest clean!

Those who passed by hurled insults at him, shaking their heads and saying, 'You who are going to destroy the temple and build it in three days, save yourself! Come down from the cross, if you are the Son of God!' (Matthew 27:39-40).

Those who passed by hurled insults at him, shaking their heads and saying, 'So! You who are going to destroy the temple and build it in three days, come down from the cross and save yourself!' (Mark 15:29-30).

The people stood watching ... (Luke 23:35a).

8.
The Passers-by

Thousands of people gathered in Jerusalem to celebrate the Passover feast. As they prepared to worship God they were unwittingly caught up in the events surrounding our Lord's crucifixion. Many, who had traced the sad procession to Calvary, stood silently watching (Luke 23:35a) — a silence that should be limited 'to the moment of the affixing to the cross and the one immediately subsequent' (Van Oosterzee). Earlier some of them had worshipped Christ, shouting, 'Hosanna to the Son of David!' (Matthew 21:9). Others, in response to Pilate's reluctance to take responsibility for Christ's death, had answered, 'Let his blood be on us and on our children!' (Matthew 27:25).

What were the attitudes and thoughts of these silent bystanders? Did the manner in which Christ suffered and his remarkable intercession soften their hearts? Did it cause them to doubt the rightness of their cries, 'Crucify him!'? Were they confused, stunned, dumbfounded by such an atrocity? Or were they unsure of what to feel or think? Maybe they had no opinion of their own. They just watched in a state of cold indifference, careless to the events that were unfolding before them. Perhaps they bowed their heads in shame, repulsed that one of their fellow countrymen was being unjustly executed, but for fear of the crowd said nothing. Dare we suggest that some, as they watched, enjoyed the spectacle, glad to see a man, who they regarded as a religious fanatic, condemned to death?

The silence was soon shattered by the jeers and accusations of the passers-by. They shook their heads in defiance and said, 'You who are going to destroy the temple and build it in three days, save yourself! Come down from the cross, if you are the Son of God!' (Matthew 27:39-40). There is little doubt that many who reproached Christ had heard him speak in parables and seen him perform the most wonderful miracles. 'They must have known that he had saved one man from an infirmity of thirty-eight years' standing; another from blindness, with which he had been afflicted from his birth; and that in a village close to Jerusalem, he had raised a dead man from the grave' (Sadler). Surely these testimonies to deity had unveiled the majesty and glory of the one hanging on the cross!

How quickly man's allegiance changes! It was only a few days ago that many in the crowd had lined the streets into Jerusalem, joyfully praising God, crying, 'Hosanna! Blessed is he who comes in the name of the Lord! Blessed is the king of Israel!' (John 12:13). Then their hopes and aspirations had been pinned on Christ. He was, or so they thought, about to deliver them from Rome's tyranny. They had believed in him and followed him. But when he was crucified all their earthly ambitions for him were torn apart and every worldly illusion shattered. So they turned their backs on him. Instead of honouring God with their praise, they insulted him by rejecting his Son; instead of raising their hands in an attitude of faithful gratitude for God's saving grace, they shook their heads in abject unbelief. They did not cry to the Saviour 'Save us!', but challenged him: 'Save yourself!' They no longer honoured their king, but exposed him to the most shameful indignity.

But why the change? Why do people in the same breath curse and bless Christ? Why do they worship him on a Sunday, and deny him in word and deed on a Monday? Why do they pray to him in the company of the religious, and blaspheme him before the profane? Why are men and women so fickle? In one sense there had been no change, for those in the crowd, like

Ben
At Holly's
3rd Birthday 1998

sheep, continued to follow one another. They were imitators, doing and saying what they thought was expected of them. They worshipped because everyone else worshipped. They shouted 'Crucify him!' because their friends shouted 'Crucify him!' They shook their heads in disgust because that is what their neighbours did. 'They had been tutored to cry, "Blessed is he who comes!" and now they were tutored to repeat what had been said at the trial about destroying the temple' (Maclaren).

Many people go astray because they are reluctant to stir up trouble by standing up for what is right. Their desire is to lead a peaceful life, so they flow with the stream, never opposing the designs of the majority. They run with the fox and hunt with the hounds, and change sides as often as they deem it prudent for their own preservation. They do not live by principle, but by fear — fear of becoming unpopular or of upsetting someone else with their views. If it pleases those around them, they cheerfully and unashamedly scorn an innocent man. Anything is permissible for them as long as it receives the applause of men.

The first insult that the onlookers fired at Christ arose from a misunderstanding and misrepresentation of his saying about the temple (John 2:19). It was an accusation that had already been levelled at him during his trial by two false witnesses (Matthew 26:61). In effect it was a challenge for Christ to prove himself: 'If you are able to destroy the temple in Jerusalem, which took forty-six years to construct (John 2:20), and build it again in three days, then prove your power by saving yourself from death!'

It requires little skill for ignorant and wicked persons to pervert the words of godly men. It is easy for them to mock what they do not understand. How many times since the first Good Friday have the words of Christ been twisted by the unscrupulous and then held up to ridicule? Such contempt is the work of Satan. He is a master at reshaping the truth so it not only preaches a different gospel, which is really no gospel at all, but sounds so improbable that it becomes laughable. On how many occasions has the Biblical account of creation been slighted and dismissed as utter nonsense by those who claim to possess superior scientific knowledge? How many have been told since childhood that the story of Adam and Eve is a fable, written by uneducated men for the amusement of us all? On the day of Pentecost, when the disciples were 'filled with the Holy Spirit and began to speak in other tongues' (Acts 2:4), there were some present who 'made fun of them and said, "They have had too much wine"' (Acts 2:13).

The second insult 'Come down from the cross, if you are the Son of God' is a deliberate and open attack on Christ's own testimony. A few hours earlier, in answer to the high priest's charge, Christ had declared himself to be the Son of God (Matthew 26:63-64). In response the Sanhedrin had accused him of blasphemy. Influenced by this, the passers-by, using the language of the devil 'if you are the Son of God' (Matthew 4:3,6), blasphemed Christ. They challenged him to prove his Sonship by coming down from the cross. Despite his all-conquering faith and absolute purity, which many of these abusers had witnessed firsthand, they despised and belittled his relationship with God and mocked his innocence. They supposed it was weakness that kept him on the cross, when really it was the strength of his love for sinners. They assumed that if he was the Son of God, God would rescue him. They failed to realise that it was 'the Lord's will to crush him and cause him to suffer' (Isaiah 53:10). They fancied that God had forsaken him because of blasphemy and other false claims. So they took up a song of derision, called by Lange, 'the most matured fruit of death.'

It is a common strategy of Satan, who always makes the most of his opportunities, to accuse and condemn us whenever God fails to answer or assist us in the way that we desire. He moves to convince us that, because divine help is not immediately forthcoming, God must have left us as orphans to face our tormentors and the trials of life. He alleges that our faith in God and his promises, if it fails to bring instant relief, is unreasonable and without purpose. It is, according to him, void of meaning and powerless to secure personal benefit.

On top of that he charges us with wrongdoing. He presents to us a myriad of sins that, he claims, have forced God from our side. But as with all Satan's 'flaming arrows' (Ephesians 6:16), it is a false charge, designed to weaken our faith and, if possible, to drive us to despair. 'Resist him,' says Peter, by 'standing firm in the faith' (1 Peter 5:9). 'Take up the shield of faith,' commands Paul, with which we can extinguish all the flames of Satan's fury (Ephesians 6:16). Never for a moment must we believe that God's delays are signs of divine indifference to our troubles, or evidences that he has abandoned his children. Never must we be deceived by the father of lies into thinking that our faith is in vain simply because God causes us to pass through the waters of affliction. If God does not respond to our cries immediately, let us submit to him nevertheless, for he is our God and Saviour, and in due time he will lift us up.

It is during seasons of spiritual oppression that we need to stand on God's word. The Scriptures are sharper than any double-edged sword and more effective by far than all the weapons of this world. There is no surer foundation to rest on, no stronger setting for our feet. When the evil one attempts to persuade us that our distresses result from God's neglect, we must counter his falsehoods by declaring in faith heaven's truth. We must appropriate with authority the words of the Psalm: 'The Lord is with me; I will not be afraid. What can man do to me? The Lord is with me; he is my helper. I will look in triumph on my enemies' (118:6-7); and take hold of such promises as: 'Never will I leave you; never will I forsake you' (Hebrews 13:5). The earth may give way around us and the mountains fall into the heart of the foaming sea, but God is always 'our refuge and strength, an ever present help in trouble' (Psalm 46:1).

In the same way the chief priests, the teachers of the law and the elders mocked him. 'He saved others,' they said, 'but he can't save himself! He's the king of Israel! Let him come down now from the cross, and we will believe in him. He trusts in God. Let God rescue him now if he wants him, for he said, "I am the Son of God."' (Matthew 27:41-43).

In the same way the chief priests and the teachers of the law mocked him among themselves. 'He saved others,' they said, 'but he can't save himself! Let this Christ, the King of Israel, come down now from the cross, that we may see and believe.' (Mark 15:31-32).

The people stood watching, and the rulers even sneered at him. They said, 'He saved others; let him save himself if he is the Christ of God, the Chosen One.' (Luke 23:35).

9.
The Sanhedrin

Blinded by a hypocritical zeal, the members of the Sanhedrin
(Nicodemus and Joseph of Arimathea excepted) behaved
contemptuously towards the Son of God. They were meant to
be 'rulers', as Luke calls them, men of dignity and principle, and
examples to the common people with whom they mingled; but
at the cross their religious masks fell away and the true
character of their hearts was discovered. From a mixture of
hatred and envy they joined the rabble in sneering at Christ
(Luke 23:35), and committed the very crime of blasphemy that
they had accused Christ of committing and which had been
used to condemn him to death.

Although both groups of men, the passers-by and the
Sanhedrin, mocked our crucified Lord, their methods were very
different. The passers-by spoke directly to Christ, insulting him
to his face. The Sanhedrin, however, displaying the character-
istics of cowards, 'mocked him among themselves' (Mark
15:31). They talked, not to him, but about him. It was as if they
were too ashamed to lift their heads to him, too guilty to look an
innocent man in the face, too afraid that he might humiliate them
with his reply, as he had done so many times before. It was
safer, so they thought, to talk behind his back. So they
whispered among themselves and voiced their derision within
earshot of Christ but with their backs turned to him.

The chief priests, the teachers of the law and the elders
were emboldened by the abuse of others to utter their own

insults. Instead of encouraging the crowd to act decently, they imitated its wickedness. Before, when asked by Jesus whether John's baptism was from heaven or from men, they would not answer according to their convictions because they were 'afraid of the people' (Matthew 21:23-27). But with Christ on the cross and the crowd on their side, they joined the scoffers and spewed out the vileness of their hearts.

The true test of the godliness and strength of a man's character is not in his ability to agree with the majority or his insistence on judging the condemned. No! It is in his undivided loyalty to Christ even in the face of many dangers. Does he stand up for Christ when the world rages against him? Is his Saviour more precious to him than the opinion of men or than his own safety? Can he remain faithful and true to what he believes when everyone else mocks and blasphemes the name he adores? Is he a light in the dark, a lone voice of love for Christ amid a hate-filled crowd?

Many professors of Christ walk merrily by his side when the warm rays of the midday sun shine down on them; but when the cold winter chill of trouble or persecution blows because of the word, they quickly fall away (Matthew 13:21). Everyone wants to own Christ as their Lord when he rides triumphantly into Jerusalem. How swiftly though do many abandon their faith when they see him on the cross! Many churchgoers want to dance without a care all the way to the pearly gates of heaven, but how many are prepared to drag their cross up the steep hills that often lead there? In a crowd that sings his praise, it is easy to join the joyful throng. It is a far harder test to remain true to our Lord in a mob that cries 'Crucify him!' When Jesus described to his disciples the events of the end times, he promised, 'All men will hate you because of me, but he who stands firm to the end will be saved' (Mark 13:13).

'He saved others', sneered these so-called religious leaders, 'but he can't save himself!' (Mark 15:31). By acknowledging that Christ 'saved others', these rulers condemned their own unbelief. If Christ had saved others, then surely, at the very least, he was worthy of the respect and dignity attributed to other good men. Why then did they treat him as if he had destroyed others? What they said about Christ was a glorious testimony to Christ, for he had indeed saved others. He had saved them from years of affliction and untold misery; from countless fears and a life of loneliness and bitterness; from a world that slowly suffocates all who follow its lusts; from the god of this world who drags his victims to an eternal damnation. Yes, Christ had saved others, but though the religious leaders paid lip-service to these miracles, unable to dismiss what their own eyes had witnessed, in their hearts they denied them.

For which miracle did they condemn Christ? Did they disapprove of the sick being healed and the demon-possessed released? Would they have preferred the blind to grope in darkness for the rest of their lives and for lepers to remain outcasts? Were they seriously accusing Jesus of wrongdoing for raising to life a widow's son or for freeing a crippled woman whom Satan had kept bound for eighteen long years? The world has gone mad when men regard good as evil and evil as good. What is astonishing about these rulers is that 'they themselves, without wishing or willing it, attested the greatness of him whom they were most deeply outraging' (Lange). They were, by the unseen power of God, involuntarily constrained to bless Christ and to pay tribute to his life of self-sacrificing love. They could find nothing worse to say against him than 'he saved others'.

Before condemning Christ they should have asked themselves: 'How does this man perform these works? By whose authority and power?' They should have listened to his own testimony when he said, 'Do not believe me unless I do what my Father does. But if I do it, even though you do not believe me, believe the miracles, that you may learn and understand that the Father is in me, and I in the Father' (John 10:37-38). But they rejected him and his miracles, viewing them as nothing more than the acts of a magician. In doing so they fulfilled what was written in their own Law: 'They hated me without reason' (John 15:24-25).

The mockers pressed home their two-pronged attack by accusing God of disowning Christ and by accusing Christ of powerlessness: 'He saved others, but he can't save himself! Let this Christ, this King of Israel, come down now from the cross, that we may see and believe' (Mark 15:31-32). Alexander remarks that 'there is peculiar venom in the sarcasm uttered by these rulers. It actually taunts him with his miracles of mercy. Without denying their reality, it exults in the supposed loss of his saving power, just when it was needed for his own deliverance.'

It is preposterous to suggest that the Son of God, who lives in the bosom of the Father and who is eternally one with him, was suddenly orphaned; or that the Christ, through whom the world was made and in whom all things hold together, was unable to save himself. He was born, not to save himself, but to save his people from their sins. How then could he abandon the cross, leaving them to perish? The Scriptures themselves, which the leaders diligently studied in the hope of possessing eternal life, testify of his vicarious sufferings and atoning death. It was not weakness that bought salvation for the Jews and Gentiles, but omnipotent love! Christ had no desire to save himself. It is through his death that men and women from every nation and walk of life are reconciled to God. 'I did not come to judge the world,' said Jesus, 'but to save it' (John 12:47). It is a blessed and eternal truth that he who 'saved others' did not save himself so that others could be saved.

The Sanhedrin's harassment of Christ, although partly stemming from a misunderstanding of the Messiah's role and kingdom, was nevertheless deliberately designed to undermine Christ's own testimony. During his trial he had spoken openly about his Messiahship. He had enraged the assembly by declaring himself to be the Son of the Blessed One, who they would see 'sitting at the right hand of the Mighty One and coming on the clouds of heaven' (Mark 14:61-62). This revelation of his divinity amounted to blasphemy in the eyes of the Sanhedrin. The problem arose because the Jews believed that the Christ was going to deliver them from Roman oppression and restore the nation of Israel to its former glory. So when Jesus was arrested and crucified by the Romans, they thought that, as he could not fulfil their Messianic hopes, he must be an impostor. By challenging him to come down from the cross they were wanting him to verify his Messianic claims as they understood them. When he did not save himself it confirmed their beliefs that he was a false Messiah.

Two questions arise at this stage: Could 'the Christ of God, the Chosen One' (Luke 23:35) have come down from the cross? And if he had, would the rulers have believed in him as they insolently claimed?

If Christ had responded to the rulers' challenge, which of course was physically possible for him, he would have saved himself, but condemned the world. He would have performed an eye-catching miracle, it is true to say, but he would not have been 'a sacrifice of atonement' (Romans 3:25) nor obedient to his Father to whom he had promised: 'I have come to do your will, O God' (Hebrews 10:7). He would have submitted to 'the spiritual forces of evil' (Ephesians 6:12) instead of 'triumphing over them by the cross' (Colossians 2:15). Nor would he have destroyed 'him who holds the power of death — that is, the devil' — or freed 'those who all their lives were held in slavery by their fear of death' (Hebrews 2:14-15). Yes, he could have come down from the cross, but in doing so he would not have satisfied the demands of the law or the justice of God.

The second question is answered by remembering that none of the other miracles performed by Jesus had convinced the Jewish leaders of his Messianic authority. Instead of believing in him on the evidence of his supernatural works, they had hardened themselves against him. They had been so infuriated by his healings on the Sabbath that they had 'plotted to arrest

Jesus in some sly way and kill him' (Matthew 26:4). Out of envy and hatred they had even made plans to kill Lazarus, whom Jesus had raised from the dead, 'for on account of him many of the Jews were going over to Jesus and putting their faith in him' (John 12:9-11). If Jesus had come down from the cross, rather than acknowledging his Messiahship, they would have accused him of performing some magical illusion and again condemned him as an evil trickster with Satanic powers.

The chief priests, the teachers of the law and the elders continued to disparage Christ among themselves and to fire their verbal arrows at him. Without realising it they adopted the language of the enemies of God's servant (Psalm 22:8), which implies that God does not care for his Son, whose faith is futile. 'He trusts in God. Let God rescue him now if he wants him, for he said, "I am the Son of God"' (Matthew 27:43). With these words they again attacked the testimony he had given to the Sanhedrin (Matthew 26:63-64). This time they insinuated that he could not be God's Son because God had not rescued him. Their logic: If Jesus is the Son of God, as he claims, then God, who loves his Son, would rescue him without delay. As it is, God has not rescued him, therefore he cannot be his Son. Lange sums up this godless conclusion by saying that 'blasphemy against Christ passes unconsciously over into blasphemy against God, for whose honour they pretend to be zealous.'

By their loud whisperings they endeavoured to tempt Christ to distrust his Father's love. This of course would have formed a rift between them. They also tried to convince any waverers who were listening that he was a deceiver and therefore unworthy of their faith. Their accusations, however, were ironic. For Christ, the Lamb 'that was slain from the creation of the world' (Revelation 13:8; cf 1 Peter 1:20), exhibited perfect trust in his Father even on the cross. It was one thing for Christ to trust in God when all men were speaking well of him. It was quite another for him to show unshaken faith in God when he was being crushed for our iniquities. And as the crucified Saviour he draws all men to himself.

The cross may be an object of ridicule to those who are perishing, but to us who are being saved it is the fountain that washes away our sins and the only door into eternal life. To some the cross is nothing more than a symbol of barbarism that displays man's inhumanity to man. To others it is a stake beneath which the burdens of guilt and sin are buried and through which all who believe are resurrected from the dead.

Our adversary the devil uses all sorts of tactics to shake our faith in God. Sometimes, especially when we are suffering grief in all kinds of trials, he cultivates doubts in our hearts about God's love for us. He endeavours to convince us of the futility of trusting in a God who allows so many problems to batter our faith. At other times he tries to condemn us, either with imaginary sins or by resurrecting sins that have long been forgiven. He may even quote Scripture at us, as he did with Christ (Matthew 4:6), or present to us an argument that, on the one hand, assures us of God's aid and protection, but on the other, accuses God of unfaithfulness when that aid and protection are not immediately forthcoming. When Christ was dying on the cross the devil hoped to weaken his faith by openly accusing his Father of rejecting the Son he claimed to love. He did not understand, at least initially, that the cross was God's way of exhibiting perfect love for sinners who had rejected him.

It must be said in connection with our passage that 'the point of truth which the devil and reprobate men can least endure is the doctrine of the Godhead of Christ. This is the rock whereupon the elect are built' (Dickson). The devil hates it when one of his former captives falls at the feet of Christ and cries, 'My Lord and my God!' (John 20:28). It is a declaration of faith that he cannot bear to hear. As the passers-by watched Christ on the cross, every effort was made by Satan to ridicule the Son of the Most High, in whom 'all the fulness of the Deity lives in bodily form' (Colossians 2:9). He wanted to persuade others to put aside any notions of this man being 'God over all' (Romans 9:5). Christ must be seen to die only as a criminal and not as the Lord of glory, before whom angels bow.

Calvin, in his summary of Christ's humiliation, says, that 'these circumstances carry great weight; for they place before us the extreme abasement of the Son of God, that we may see more clearly how much our salvation cost him. And that, reflecting that we justly deserved all the punishments which he endured, we may be more and more excited to repentance. For in this exhibition God has plainly showed to us how wretched our condition would have been, if we had not a Redeemer.' If your sins have not yet been forgiven, then consider him who endured such opposition from sinful men. Survey the cross on which the prince of glory died. See how he poured out his life and suffered untold agonies. Go to Calvary with a humble and contrite spirit and be washed in the precious blood of Christ, the lamb without blemish or defect. Lay low at the foot of that cursed tree and behold the Redeemer, who receives all who come to him. Reach out to him in faith and be reconciled to God.

In the same way the robbers who were crucified with him also heaped insults on him. (Matthew 27:44).

Those crucified with him also heaped insults on him. (Mark 15:32b).

One of the criminals who hung there hurled insults at him: 'Aren't you the Christ? Save yourself and us!'

But the other criminal rebuked him. 'Don't you fear God,' he said, 'since you are under the same sentence? We are punished justly, for we are getting what our deeds deserve. But this man has done nothing wrong.'

Then he said, 'Jesus, remember me when you come into your kingdom.'

Jesus answered him, 'I tell you the truth, today you will be with me in paradise.' (Luke 23:39-43).

10.
The Two Robbers

The two criminals, who were justly condemned for their crimes, even in their dying hours, 'heaped insults' on the Son of God (Matthew 27:44). With their last breath they cursed the God who made them, and vilified him who was enduring such agonies for their sake. Why in their extremity did they abuse the only one who could save them from eternal damnation, a fate far worse than crucifixion? Were they despising Christ for his innocency? Were they mocking him because he had the authority of a king?

Christ made no reply to the accusations, challenges and blasphemies that were hurled in his face — he shouted no rebuke at his enemies, uttered no threat and offered no excuse; 'instead, he entrusted himself to him who judges justly' (1 Peter 2:22-23). There was no better time for him to obey his own injunction: 'Do not give dogs what is sacred; do not throw your pearls to pigs. If you do, they may trample them under feet, and then turn and tear you to pieces' (Matthew 7:6). If Christ had answered his accusers, would they have listened? Would they have stopped their taunting and taken up a song of praise to God? Would they have fallen on their knees under the burden of their shameful indignities and, in the shadow of the cross, confessed their sins to the Most High? No doubt, in keeping with the inclinations of their hearts, they would have sunk to lower levels of contempt.

'One of the criminals who hung there hurled insults at him: "Aren't you the Christ? Save yourself and us!"' (Luke 23:39). The wicked heart cannot be tamed by tortures. It is hard like iron, and unbending under the rod of affliction. 'Straits and torment will not tame a reprobate. Even on the threshold of hell he will blaspheme God, without a cause offered' (Dickson). Punishments and suffering, without grace, are not sufficient to convert a soul. In themselves they will stiffen the resolve and further harden the heart against the cross of Christ. 'The fire that softens gold only hardens clay' (Van Doren). A view of death, unaided by the regenerating power of God's Spirit, never leads to repentance or humbles a proud spirit. The arrogant march on, regardless of the troubles that burden them, and the dying use the final hours of life to convince themselves that there is no God to answer, no hell to escape, no Saviour to adore.

The impenitent thief felt no dread of God's judgment and desired no mercy. He even sneered at the Christ who could have answered his petition, if sincere. Without a thought that Christ could 'save' him, not from the cross, but from eternal damnation, he foamed out blasphemies. He tormented the Saviour of sinners and insulted the Christ of God. What irony that he should challenge Christ to save his body, when Christ could have saved his soul! What ignorance from a man who had no idea that his mocking cry for his accomplice would soon be heard! What frightening obstinacy from a condemned wretch, not only hanging on a cross, but hanging over hell!

The truly repentant man does not snarl at Christ, but weeps before him in brokenness of spirit. He does not point an accusing finger in his face, but bows his head and beats his breast, crying, 'God, have mercy on me, a sinner' (Luke 18:13). He may use the same words as the crucified criminal: 'Save me!', but the tone is one of humble faith in the God of mercy. Rather than demanding salvation from God as his right, he pleads with God, as an undeserving sinner, to have mercy upon his soul for the sake of Christ. He presumes nothing, but believes that 'all things are possible with God' (Mark 10:27).

It is not *what* we say to God that counts, but *how* we say it. We might utter the most eloquent confession imaginable, perfect in tone and Biblical expression, but if it does not come from a heart humbled by the Spirit of God, it will not be answered. If, on the other hand, we stumble through a prayer of repentance, devastated at the sight of our own vileness and yet hopeful of God's grace, our prayer shall be heard and our sins washed away by Christ's blood. It may hurt to acknowledge the truth about ourselves, but it will move the Sun of Righteousness to rise with healing in his wings.

The other malefactor, who at first railed against Christ along with everyone else (Matthew 27:44), turned and rebuked his partner in crime: 'Don't you fear God,' he said, 'since you are under the same sentence? We are punished justly, for we are getting what our deeds deserve. But this man has done nothing wrong' (Luke 23:40-41). He stopped insulting an enemy and started to support a friend.

What led to this sudden and unexpected transformation? What were the means that God employed to wrest another sinner from Satan's grasp? The Bible is silent on the matter so we can only conjecture. It could be that before his arrest this robber had heard Christ preach and witnessed some of his miracles. Then on the cross these divine words and works were resurrected in his mind and strikingly forced home to his conscience. Perhaps he was so impressed with the composed and divine-like behaviour of his dying neighbour amidst the jeering multitude that he felt compelled to confess Christ as Lord. Or was it the cry 'Father, forgive' that tore the veil from his heart, enabling him to embrace Christ as the Lamb of God, or the words of the superscription that hung above Christ's head that enlightened his soul? We do not know the means God used to change his mind, but this new conviction moved him to rebuke his partner for displaying an utter disregard for the judgement of God. Both men were condemned justly and about to stand before the eternal Judge: one trembled at the prospect, the other showed no remorse or fear.

The penitent malefactor preached from the cross a sermon that all generations should hear. It was a sermon of confession from a man who knew he had sinned grievously and fallen short of God's glory. With straightforward honesty, he acknowledged his sin, openly and without any attempt to disguise or excuse it. He admitted he had failed to meet God's demands and was therefore worthy of damnation. Yet, at the same time, like all true penitents, he threw himself on Christ in the hope of mercy. It was also a sermon that heralded the innocency of Christ.

The robber recognised that while he was punished justly, the man hanging next to him was suffering without cause. 'He has done nothing wrong!' was the exclamation to his accomplice. Throughout the ages men and women have often accused Christ of iniquity; yet, despite their most strenuous efforts, they have never proved him guilty of sin. Even Pilate, a cynical and callous Roman governor, found no basis for any charges against him, agreeing with his wife that Jesus was an 'innocent man' (Matthew 27:19).

It was a remarkable sermon, for with a few simple words the robber proclaimed some of the foundational truths of the gospel: the wickedness of fallen man, the spotlessness of Christ, and God's grace to sinners. In our natural state the judgement against us reads: 'There is no one righteous, not even one; there is no one who understands, no one who seeks God. All have turned away, they have together become worthless' (Romans 3:10-12). But thanks be to God, for by his grace he opens our eyes to see Christ, a Saviour majestic in holiness and worthy of unending praise, and crucified for our sakes, that we might exchange the deserved agonies of hell for the free gift of eternal life.

It is amazing grace that saves to the uttermost the worst of men! We may be the chief of sinners, having lived a life of debauchery and crime unparalleled by our contemporaries. We may have shamed our parents, disgusted our friends and been rejected as vile and hopeless by those who have tried to help us.

We may have uttered unmentionable blasphemies against God and treated his servants with such scorn that even those who do not fear God have wondered why divine wrath has not consumed us. But thanks be to God — Christ died for men and women like us. He came, not to call the healthy, but to heal the sick. He died to free those bound by the chains of depravity and to save sinners who cry out to him for mercy. It is only divine love that reaches down to save and that freely blots out transgressions.

The disciples had denied and forsaken Christ, but God had reserved a condemned thief to recognise the glory of his Son and to be an example to the world of his saving grace. At the cross he ceased shouting insults at Christ and turned to face his Saviour with a humble dependence that shamed the watching crowd. 'Jesus,' he said, 'remember me when you come into your kingdom' (Luke 23:42). With these words he displayed a clearer perception of the reality of Christ's kingdom than any of the disciples had shown. With them he 'became a herald of the royal dignity of our Lord, in the same instant in which the Messianic hope of the apostles themselves was most vehemently shaken' (Van Oosterzee). He did not ask to be liberated from the suffering of crucifixion, but cast himself on the unlimited mercy of Christ. He wanted to be remembered by Christ when he returned in royal glory to set up his everlasting kingdom. He knew it was an eternal and spiritual kingdom that was founded on the cross, and that Jesus was its supreme head. For as he had watched Christ he had seen, through the eyes of faith, 'life in death, exaltation in ruin, glory in shame, victory in destruction, and a kingdom in bondage' (Calvin).

The robber 'adored Christ as a King while on the gallows, celebrated his kingdom in the midst of shocking and worse than revolting abasement, and declared him, when dying, to be the Author of life' (ibid.). How much more then should we who are alive and well, and foreigners to persecution, bow with reverence and awe before the throne of the **KING OF KINGS.** The robber elevated Christ, whose form was 'marred beyond human likeness' (Isaiah 52:14) and whose life was poured out unto death. In the light of his example should we not exalt the ascended Christ who is arrayed with eternal splendour and seated at the right hand of the Majesty in heaven? If the robber exercised faith in Christ when he was 'despised and rejected by men' (Isaiah 53:3), what excuse do we have for not trusting wholeheartedly in the risen Saviour who is worshipped by countless thousands the world over? If a crucified robber took such pains to preach the righteousness of Christ, is it too much for us to uphold the glories of our Lord?

If we are not Christians, perhaps we are tempted by the robber's last minute conversion to delay our own repentance until the final hour of life. But when will that hour be? It may occur in ten years' time or in a month from now. If our lives are spared for another twenty-five years, what will be the state of our hearts before God then? What makes us think that if we are stalling now, we shall not be stalling then? If we are apologising for our unbelief today, it is a sure fact that we shall still be apologising tomorrow, unless God intervenes. Time does not change the heart or disposition. A thousand millennia could pass, but we shall be no nearer accepting Christ than on the day of our birth. Time alone offers no improvement to the soul. So turn to Christ now, in obedience to his command, for 'now is the time of God's favour, and now is the day of salvation' (2 Corinthians 6:2).

The two robbers furnish us with the two different ways that sinners meet eternity. The first, insolent and proud, refused to allow the torments of this world to aid him escape the torments of the next. He used his dying moments, not to implore God for mercy, but to curse the God he had for years despised. The second, though his life had been as wretched and as dishonouring to God as the first, fell in faith upon Christ, his only hope. He acted upon the promise that opens the door of life to the unworthy: 'Everyone who calls on the name of the Lord will be saved' (Acts 2:21).

Our Lord 'did not open his mouth' (Isaiah 53:7) in response to the blasphemies of his enemies, but as soon as he heard the penitent's petition he answered with the words, 'I tell you the truth, today you will be with me in paradise' (Luke 23:43). Even on the cross Christ received sinners kindly and immediately. This word to the thief is Christ's second saying from the cross. His first is a plea for forgiveness, the second is a promise of glorification. The first is a prayer on behalf of his enemies, the second a word of assurance to a newborn friend. It is a word that demonstrates the power and authority Christ possesses to save sinners. It unveils his willingness to open heaven's door to all who knock on it. It is a word that 'turns the stake of the cross into a throne of grace' (Van Doren) and 'comprehends, in a short summary, the whole riches and glory of redemption. The first word on the cross gives us a view into his high-priestly heart. His kingly character reveals itself in the second. Grace and majesty suddenly diffuse their bright beams through the night of the deepest humiliation' (Van Oosterzee).

The thief, not daring to presume too much, asked to be remembered by Christ in the distant and remote future. Christ, who is so willing to hear and answer our petitions, and who is able to do immeasurably more than all we ask or imagine, secured his eternal destiny 'today', that is, before the sun disappeared over the horizon. The thief did not have to be baptised to be saved or to partake in the communion. He did not have to pass through a religious ritual or to be put on probation. He did not have to grapple with a series of penances or dwell for a time in purgatory. He only had to exercise a child-like faith in Christ and express a deep sorrow for sin. That was enough for him to enter, immediately upon death, the paradise of God. A few hours later the soldiers, in order to hasten death, came and broke the legs of the two criminals (John 19:32), who would otherwise have hung on their crosses for two or three days. Thus they inadvertently fulfilled in a literal sense Christ's prophecy: 'Today you will be with me in paradise'.

Death holds no terrors for those who rest in Christ. The apostle Paul sums up the believer's attitude when he says, 'For to me, to live is Christ and to die is gain' and to depart and be with Christ is 'better by far' (Philippians 1:21,23). It is a moment of glorious triumph when a Christian lays down his arms and puts off the body of sin. It is heaven itself when he no longer looks at 'a poor reflection', but sees 'face to face' and knows fully, even as he is fully known (1 Corinthians 13:12). When he turns his back once and for all on the temptations of this world and says a final farewell to the tears of sorrow, he satisfies his heart's desire and gains the hope of glory. But above all else, for him to dwell in the presence of his Saviour throughout eternity is the prize for which his soul most yearns. 'With me' were the sweetest words that the robber heard from the lips of our Lord. What joy to abide in the bosom of Christ our friend and lover for countless ages to come! What a reward to dwell in the presence of him who is fairer than ten thousand and the jewel in every crown! Who compares with or outshines his glory? Paradise is only paradise because it is the home of the Saviour we adore.

The promise of Christ was glorious in that it restored and healed the robber's soul; but it did not, nor was it designed to, alleviate his present suffering. The work of God must never be judged by our physical state. Our body may be racked with constant pain, with every movement causing us to cry out, but that is no reason to think that God is not near or that his blessing has departed. Afflictions, if they are used aright, are aids that prepare our hearts to meet with God. On the other hand, if peace and health are our daily friends, never leaving or forsaking us, how foolish we should be to imagine that our temporal ease is a sure sign of God's presence with us. Times of tranquillity assure us of God's general and overall care for his creatures. They are not deposits guaranteeing salvation.

One final thought. Which of the two robbers is a mirror to our own souls? When we hear of Christ, the King of the Jews, dying on the cross, what is our reaction? What thoughts flood our minds? What feelings rise in our hearts? Do we silently scoff at the foolishness of it? Do we wonder why he did not save himself if he was the Son of God, or at least silence the mocking crowd with some miraculous deed? Do we challenge him to prove his Sonship, promising to believe if he will show his power to us? Or do we beat our breasts in shame, stunned at the price he had to pay for our salvation? Are we ready to utter our thanks to him for being 'pierced for our transgressions' and 'crushed for our iniquities' (Isaiah 53:5)? Do we bow at his feet and shed tears of godly sorrow, knowing that it is only through the cross that the gates of paradise open for the oppressed and broken-hearted? Do we marvel at God's sacrificial love for the unworthy? Which of the two robbers do we follow? Do we taunt or do we repent? Are you a sinner without hope or a sinner saved by grace?

Near the cross of Jesus stood his mother, his mother's sister, Mary the wife of Clopas, and Mary of Magdala. When Jesus saw his mother there, and the disciple whom he loved standing near by, he said to his mother, 'Dear woman, here is your son,' and to the disciple, 'Here is your mother.' From that time on, this disciple took her into his home. (John 19:25-27).

11.
The Two Marys and the Disciple whom Jesus Loved

'Near the cross of Jesus stood his mother, his mother's sister, Mary the wife of Clopas, and Mary of Magdala' (John 19:25). A group of faithful women stood near the cross, offering our Lord and Saviour whatever succour they could — tender looks, an assuring presence, abiding support. They were determined to remain true to Christ despite the seething mob whose blasphemies resounded in their ears. How could they forsake the one they loved! Their affection for him was too deep, their faith in him too strong. He was their rose of Sharon in whom they rejoiced, their Lord and Master for whom they were prepared to grieve unto death. 'Thus in the midst of rage and fury, love stands near Jesus in his dying moments. It lifts up to him its tearful and affectionate eye. Behold a lovely little company in the midst of Belial, a hidden rose-bud under wild and tangled bramble-bushes, a splendid wreath of lilies around the death-bed of the Redeemer' (Krummacher).

These women separated themselves from the others, who were 'watching from a distance' (Matthew 27:55), and drew near to the cross. Their faith in and love for Christ, though sorely tested, compelled them to move closer to the cursed tree. From Galilee they had followed Christ and supported him out of their own means. On Calvary, when he needed them most, they stood by him, mindful of their duty and faithful to their friend.

They had been changed by his love for them, a love that had washed and renewed them, and filled their hearts with the desires of heaven. So out of love for him and a gratitude for all he had done, they drew near to uphold their dying Saviour. Love is as 'strong as death' and as 'unyielding as the grave. It burns like blazing fire, like a mighty flame. Many waters cannot quench love; rivers cannot wash it away' (Song of Songs 8:6-7). Christ was stripped of his dignity by ruthless men, and condemned and crucified by the unjust, yet these women of faith remained true to him throughout.

One of the women who stood near the cross was Mary of Magdala, out of whom Jesus had driven seven demons (Mark 16:9). She was also present at the tomb when Jesus was buried (Matthew 27:61); among the group of women who, very early on the third day, took spices to the tomb in order 'to anoint Jesus' body' (Mark 16:1); and she was the first person to whom Jesus appeared after his resurrection (Mark 16:9). All of this testifies that the work of grace wrought in her life had not been in vain. By following Christ, first to the cross and then to the tomb, she proved her deep affection for him and produced the fruit of love and gratitude that are acceptable to God.

God does not want a sterile, formal religion that is bound to duty for conscience's sake, but a life of devotion and thankfulness that stems from a vital union with his Son. He delights, not in sacrifices that are reluctantly offered, but in an obedience and love that flow from the springs of salvation. Mary of Magdala did not have to be forced or cajoled into following Christ, first to the cross and then to the tomb. So great was her love for him that no one could stop her. She was unafraid of the dangers of publicly supporting a condemned man, unhindered by personal grief, unperturbed by what others would think. She loved Christ, and for her that demanded faithfulness to the end.

If only more men and women were compelled by the love of Christ! If only the cold, hard hearts that adore the traditions of men would melt and overflow with the joys of salvation and burst with rivers of living waters! If only the lukewarmness that cripples so many saints would become red hot zeal, fervent for God's glory! Then the lifelessness that fills so many meeting-houses would be replaced by an unquenchable passion for the things of God, and an army of Christians would be ready to march forth into Satan's territory, proclaiming freedom for the captives.

What is the difference between Mary of Magdala and many believers? After Jesus had been anointed by a sinful woman who, much to the disgust of Simon the Pharisee, wet Jesus' feet with her tears and then wiped them with her hair and kissed them, he said, 'I tell you, her many sins have been forgiven — for she loved much. But he who has been forgiven little loves little' (Luke 7:47). Mary of Magdala knew the depth of the pit from which Jesus had rescued her. She knew how tightly she had been bound by Satan's chains before the hand of divine mercy had set her free. She had been forgiven much and so, from a heart overwhelmed by gratitude for God's grace, she loved her Saviour much. Many Christians only dimly see the mire of death from which they have been snatched. It is as if they know the truth in their heads but have never been awestruck by it in their hearts. They have been told the cost of their salvation, but have never counted that cost for themselves. They have read about the vileness of the human heart, but have failed to see the extent of that vileness in their own hearts. They love little because they think they have been forgiven little. Thus the flame of God's Spirit is all but extinguished.

The other woman at the cross we must mention is Mary, the mother of Jesus. She too stood near to the one she loved, undaunted by the clamour around her. 'Neither her own danger, nor the sadness of the spectacle, nor the insults of the crowd, could restrain her from performing the last office of duty and tenderness to her Divine Son on the cross' (Doddridge). With a holy dignity she exercised her motherly instincts and supported to the end our dying Saviour. As she watched the awful scene unfold, Simon's prophecy, uttered over thirty years before, must have shaken her: 'And a sword will pierce your own soul too' (Luke 2:35). Little had she known just how sharp that sword would be or how deep it would penetrate. Surely there is nothing more grievous for a mother than to see her own son, whom she has nursed and nurtured with such care, butchered by men so callous.

The grief of Mary was unimaginable, the pain indescribable, yet with what fortitude and composure she suffered! There were no hysterics or wild gestures. There were no outcries against the mob or hate-filled demonstrations against the authorities responsible for crucifying her son. She heard the cruel insults of the crowd and the hypocrisy of the chief priests; she saw the soldiers casting lots for Christ's clothes; she watched her beloved son writhing in pain, bleeding, dying; yet she did not forsake her post. She suffered quietly and with great dignity.

'When Jesus saw his mother there, and the disciple whom he loved standing nearby, he said to his mother, "Dear woman, here is your son," and to the disciple, "Here is your mother." From that time on, this disciple took her into his home' (John 19:26-27). There was no self-pity exhibited by Christ, no yearning for sympathy. Even at the hour of sacrifice he cared for others more than he cared for himself. He comforted the bereaved. 'Though horrible blasphemies against God filled his mind with inconceivable grief, and though he sustained a dreadful contest with eternal death and with the devil, still, none of these things prevented him from being anxious about his mother' (Calvin). It is so easy, during times of trial, to forget everyone except ourselves. We become the centre of our own attention. We demand that others turn their sympathies towards our cause. Our need is the focus, our comfort the aim, our uplifting the priority. With Jesus it was always others first. He did not plead with his murderers to have mercy on him, but prayed for their forgiveness. He did not contest his innocence with the robbers, but reached out to one of them in love. He did not command his mother to fight for his release, but gently placed her in the care of the disciple whom he loved.

When Jesus saw his mother, distressed and broken, his heart went out to her, as it had done to so many people before. He reached out to her in compassion, as a son performing one final duty to his beloved mother, and as a Saviour, who watches over the elect 'to the very end of the age'(Matthew 28:20). As her son he met her temporal and immediate needs by giving her John, a substitute son. As her Saviour he provided her with a further demonstration of his boundless and ever-faithful love. Oh that we might have power 'to grasp how wide and long and high and deep is the love of Christ, and to know this love that surpasses knowledge' (Ephesians 4:18-19)! How light and momentary would our troubles appear, if we caught a glimpse of Christ's redeeming love! To see him, torn in body and crushed for our sins, yet more concerned for our welfare and salvation than for his own deliverance — what salve for a wounded soul! Who in their right mind could sneer at such grace or reject so great a Saviour?

Much has been written about why Jesus addressed his mother as 'Dear woman' and not as Mary. Some think that Jesus, ever careful with his words, did not want to pierce his mother with a deeper wound by referring to her by name. The name 'Mary' was too personal for such an occasion, too heart-breaking for his mother to hear. The general title 'woman' was less likely to evoke an emotional response. A better interpretation is to say that Christ exhorted his mother not to think of him merely as her son, but as her Saviour and Lord, who is equally bound to all sinners. He was about to die and to go to his Father, where he would be above all earthly relations. She had to learn to put no confidence in the flesh or in her special relationship to Christ, but to humble herself before him, confessing her sins, with the knowledge that it is only those who 'do the will of my Father in heaven' who are counted members of the family of God (Matthew 12:50). Suffering for her son had to become subservient to suffering for her Lord.

There are many people who put confidence in things that are worthless as far as salvation is concerned: upbringing, nationality, morality, knowledge, religion, reputation, good works. The Pharisees diligently studied the Scriptures, thinking that by them they could possess eternal life; yet they rejected the Christ about whom the Scriptures testify (John 5:39). It is vain and blasphemous to regard anything except Christ and his death as sufficient for salvation. Some of the things mentioned above have their good points and are beneficial in some areas, but they earn no merit before a holy God. It is only the crucified Lord who has the authority to forgive sins.

How sad that many Christians, like the Galatians, after starting on the road of life by trusting wholeheartedly in Christ, are distracted by the trappings of religion. After beginning with the Spirit, they try to attain their goal by human effort (Galatians 3:3). These 'extras' are nothing more than entanglements that trip us up as we run the race marked out for us. They must never be allowed to suffocate our faith in the sufficiency of Christ or to deceive others into thinking that the blood of the Lamb fails to satisfy the justice of God.

Jesus also saw John standing by his mother's side. John was 'the disciple whom Jesus loved' and the one who had 'leaned back against Jesus at the supper and said, "Lord, who is going to betray you?" ' (John 21:20). He was the 'other disciple' who had brought Peter into the high priest's courtyard (John 18:15-16) and the only one of the twelve who had followed the Lord to Calvary. Christ's love for John evoked love from John; hence he was found standing near the cross. With calm assurance Jesus spoke first to his mother and then to John. Chrysostom notes 'how imperturbable our Lord is during his crucifixion, talking to John and his mother, fulfilling prophecies, giving good hope to the thief; whereas, before his crucifixion, he seemed in fear. The weakness of his nature was shown there, the exceeding greatness of his power here.'

When Jesus saw John he committed his mother into his care. 'What an amazing privilege! Thus to have been appointed by the Incarnate Word himself to supply his place towards his bereaved mother! How stupendous a legacy was this for divine piety to bequeath, and for adoring love to inherit!' (Lange). God honours those who honour him and 'whoever can be trusted with very little can also be trusted with much' (Luke 16:10). John was faithful in supporting Christ to the end, undaunted by the cost of discipleship, uninfluenced by the actions of his dearest friends. As a result he was entrusted with the responsibility of looking after Mary and exalted into the same earthly family as our Lord.

If we cannot be trusted with someone else's property, should we expect property of our own? If we are dishonest with worldly wealth, who will trust us with true riches? When an acquaintance steals the small change we left on the table, it would not be wise to ask him to deposit large sums of money in our bank! If a friend finds it impossible to fulfil the daily duties of life, we are hardly likely to recommend him for an important post in the king's army. Common sense alone dictates a measure of caution towards the unreliable. On the other hand, if someone performs with enthusiasm and honesty the menial tasks assigned to him, we can feel confident that he will engage in more noble work with equal vigour and uprightness. If he is careful to love and protect other people's children, then God will give him children of his own. The apostle John had proved over the years he had spent with Jesus that he was a man of principle and integrity. Therefore Christ had no hesitation in committing Mary to his care. John, for his part, readily obeyed Christ's command, for 'from that time on, this disciple took her into his home' (John 19:27).

Many women were there, watching from a distance. They had followed Jesus from Galilee to care for his needs. Among them were Mary Magdalene, Mary the mother of James and Joseph, and the mother of Zebedee's sons. (Matthew 27:55-56).

Some women were watching from a distance. Among them were Mary Magdalene, Mary the mother of James the younger and of Joses, and Salome. In Galilee these women had followed him and cared for his needs. Many other women who had come up with him to Jerusalem were also there. (Mark 15:40-41).

But all those who knew him, including the women who had followed him from Galilee, stood at a distance, watching these things. (Luke 23:49).

12.
The Women at the Cross

Mark in his Gospel says that 'some women were watching from a distance. Among them were Mary Magdalene, Mary the mother of James the younger and of Joses, and Salome. In Galilee these women had followed him and cared for his needs. Many other women who had come up with him to Jerusalem were also there' (Mark 15:40-41). These devoted women, some of whom had already performed an honourable duty to our Saviour in providing for his needs, portrayed a rare courage as they remained unshaken in their fidelity to Christ. They were not like fair-weather friends, who stand near to Christ when the pleasant breezes of popularity and prosperity blow, but are strangely absent when storm clouds rise. Nor were they akin to those 'who receive the word with joy when they hear it, but have no root. They believe for a while, but in the time of testing they fall away' (Luke 8:13). These women had hearts filled with a love and sympathy for Christ that overcame their deepest fears and empowered them to resist the severest temptation.

The women at the cross are a silent rebuke to the disciples. 'Peter wanders lonesomely about. The other scattered sheep have vanished, without leaving a trace, when the Shepherd was smitten. Only the faithfulness of female love holds its ground when all seems lost' (Van Oosterzee). The men ran from Christ, the women drew near. The men, out of fear, cowered away in some dark corner to protect themselves; the women,

though fearful, stood in the open to proclaim their devotion to
Christ. The men fainted, the women followed. The men
succumbed to the weakness of the flesh; the women, supported
by the power of God, triumphed over their natural frailties. It is
not the strength of the body that prevails against temptation, but
the power of faith.

The courage of these women shamed Peter, who had
confidently boasted: 'Even if I have to die with you, I will never
disown you' (Matthew 26:35). It is one thing to proclaim our
faithfulness to Christ in the privacy of our rooms, when danger
or persecution is unseen; it is another to act with undivided
loyalty in the face of public hostility. Any Christian, moved by
the emotion of the hour, is capable of uttering strong sentiments
of loyalty and devotion to Christ. How many, though, when
threatened with the fiery furnace, can repeat the words of
Shadrach, Meshach and Abednego: 'The God we serve is able
to save us from it, and he will rescue us from your hand, O king.
But even if he does not, we want you to know, O king, that we
will not serve your gods or worship the image of gold you have
set up' (Daniel 3:17-18). Actions speak louder than words and
are a surer test of the genuineness of faith (1 Peter 1:7).

The presumption of Peter provides all of us with a warning:
'If you think you are standing firm, be careful that you don't fall'
(1 Corinthians 10:12). We may imagine that our faith is
invincible and our love for Christ stronger than death, but unless
we depend solely on God, we shall not be able to stand when
the day of evil comes. It is not faith itself that fortifies our hearts,
but the author of faith. It is not love on its own that fits us to resist
temptation, but the Lord whom we love. He is the one who
shields us from the terror of night and the arrows that fly by day.
It is under his wing that we find refuge. The women at the cross
were not trusting in their own religious beliefs and affections,
but in Christ. They had learned to fix their eyes on Jesus, 'the
author and perfecter of our faith' (Hebrews 12:2), and to adore
him, the lover of their souls. So if we boast of 'standing firm'

when we are not feasting upon God and his promises or delighting in his Son, we are on shaky ground. If we are placing our confidence solely in human will-power and effort, we are bound to fall. We shall be like Peter, whose words and actions contradicted each other.

One final comment should be made about these women. Before following Christ to Calvary, they had already spent a number of years cheerfully providing for him. This service had not been a token gesture, grudgingly offered, but a life of sacrificial giving out of their own property, which culminated in the giving of themselves at the cross. They were like the poor widow who put two very small copper coins into the temple treasury, which was 'all she had to live on' (Luke 21:4). As Christians, our dedication to Christ must never be half-hearted or reluctant. It is a poor testimony of God's love and power to see someone who professes Christ miserably performing their duty to him. Our service should be as willing as his sacrifice, and our commitment to him similar to his obedience to God. Then what we bring to him will be 'a fragrant offering, an acceptable sacrifice, pleasing to God' (Philippians 4:18).

The Death

From the sixth hour until the ninth hour darkness came over all the land. (Matthew 27:45).

At the sixth hour darkness came over the whole land until the ninth hour. (Mark 15:33).

It was now about the sixth hour, and darkness came over the whole land until the ninth hour, for the sun stopped shining. (Luke 23:44-45a).

13.
Darkness

Jesus had already been on the cross for three hours when 'from the sixth hour until the ninth hour darkness came over all the land' (Matthew 27:45). This darkness, which began at twelve o'clock (noon), the halfway point of Christ's sufferings, was both dramatic and unforgettable: it occurred in the middle of the day, when the sun is at its highest and brightest; it lasted for three consecutive hours; and it covered the 'whole land' (Mark 15:33). Because of it men and women could not go about their normal business, children had to cease their games and those standing by the cross were blinded to the agonies of our Saviour. Jerusalem, normally a hive of activity, came to a standstill. Its citizens, up to then unperturbed by the death of another 'criminal', were forced to reflect: 'Why has this deep and terrible darkness descended upon us? What is its meaning? Have we defiled our way and aroused divine wrath? Could that man on the cross, for whose death we accepted full responsibility (Matthew 27:25), really be God's Son?'

One question that many have tried to answer is: What caused the darkness? Some, in an attempt to explain it away, describe various natural phenomena that could have caused it, such as a three hour thunderstorm, an eclipse of the sun, or the atmospheric changes that sometimes precede earthquakes. An eclipse of the sun can be ruled out straightaway, because the Passover was always celebrated at the time of the full moon when an eclipse of the sun is impossible. Besides, eclipses only last a few minutes. A thunderstorm or some atmospheric or cosmic cause, even if it had lasted three hours, could not have produced darkness 'over all the land' or been referred to by the Gospel writers without gross exaggeration. Luke simply states that 'the sun stopped shining' (23:45). This short statement highlights the depth and intensity of the darkness as well as its supernatural cause; for it was God who blotted out the sun. He cut off its rays from Christ, the 'light of the world' (John 8:12). At Christ's birth the glory of the Lord brightened the night sky (Luke 2:9), at his death darkness shrouded the day.

Another question that is often asked in connection with this supernatural darkness is: How extensive was it? That is, did it cover the whole earth or just the land of Israel? Matthew, Mark and Luke all say it came over the whole land (27:45; 15:33; 23:44). This limits the darkness to the nation of Israel, the people to whom Jesus was sent. Although this interpretation is restrictive, it nevertheless emphasises the miraculous character of the darkness and points more definitely to the people of Israel who, 'with the help of wicked men, put Jesus to death by nailing him to the cross' (Acts 2:23). It was as if God, by a supernatural act, was drawing attention to the nation that 'killed the author of life' (Acts 3:15).

A third and far more important question is: What does it mean? Why did darkness envelop the Son of God for the last three hours of his life? Some believe that God, whose 'eyes are too pure to look on evil' (Habakkuk 1:13), was hiding his face from the most heinous of crimes — the crucifixion of his beloved Son. As the Father he could not bear the hideous spectacle of his Son's torture any longer. Others interpret the sign more metaphorically. They say that Christ's sacrifice was so crucial to the salvation of sinners and so world-changing that it was as if the sun, in recognition of its importance, fell out of the heavens. The sun bowed down to the Son of God, whose glory far outshines its own, and closed its eyes to the terrors of sin that were laid on him, unable to witness the wrath of God consuming the Lord of heaven and earth. Others say it depicts, somewhat symbolically, the death of the sun of righteousness and the extinguishing of the 'light of men' (John 1:4). Still others refer it to the blinding of the nation of Israel. Just as the Jews rejected Christ, so God deprived them of the light that shines in the darkness. Instead of seeing 'the glory of the one and only Son, who came from the Father, full of grace and truth' (John 1:14), they were handed over to the darkness of despair and destruction.

What is clear from this sign is that God was assuring 'those who would receive it of something exceedingly terrible in itself, and exceedingly momentous to us, that was going on in the invisible and spiritual world' (Sadler). Through the darkness God was demonstrating his justice to a lost and fallen world, whose sins he had previously left unpunished (Romans 3:25). He was visibly manifesting his anger against Christ, 'the atoning sacrifice for our sins' (1 John 2:2). Divine wrath, as it were, burned 'itself out in the very heart of Jesus, so that he, as our substitute, suffered the most intense agony, indescribable woe and terrible isolation. Hell came to Calvary that day, and the Saviour descended into it and bore its horrors in our stead' (Hendriksen).

The darkness heralds God's intense hatred of sin and the necessity of satisfying divine justice. There are those who delude themselves into thinking that God is only a God of love. They say he either ignores sin altogether, never demanding a payment for it, or he somehow regards the guilty as innocent, though their debts have never been paid. But to trust in a God who is careless about sin and who fails to visit sinners with just punishments, is to live in a world of make-believe where right is wrong and wrong is right. It is to live where a holy and righteous God does not reign. The sufferings of Christ and the damned in hell both announce with loud cries the abhorrence of God towards sin. In fact, the moral government of the world and the testimonies of our own consciences should be sufficient for us to echo the words of the Psalmist: 'You are not a God who takes pleasure in evil; with the wicked you cannot dwell. The arrogant cannot stand in your presence; you hate all who do wrong. You destroy those who tell lies; bloodthirsty and deceitful men the Lord abhors' (Psalm 5:4-6). Would a God who is indifferent to wrongdoing have crushed his own Son for our iniquities? Would he have pierced him through for our transgressions or cast the ungodly into endless torment if sin was something he could overlook?

Let the darkness that enveloped the Lamb of God on the cross sound a warning to those who play with sin, regarding it as a trifle and as a pleasure not to be denied. May it cause them to forsake their way and flee to Christ, who alone can save them from blackest darkness. At Calvary sin was blotted out, death was dealt a fatal blow, and God's love for the world was manifested. So why continue in sin? It is against all reason. Do you imagine that because your sins are only petty in your own eyes that you will never have to pay the price for them? Are you pretending that when you stand before the bar of God you will be able to convince him of your worthiness of eternal life? Come to your senses and close your account with God at Calvary. Have your name cleared by bathing in the blood of Christ. Stretch forth your hand and touch him who is able to clothe you in the garments of righteousness. Come out of the darkness of guilt and condemnation and into the light of heavenly glory.

The darkness also speaks a word of hope to the despondent, who are weighed down by the burden of their own sin and whose sense of justice declares that there is no forgiveness. It is true that without Christ there would be no light at the end of sin's tunnel. But thanks be to God, sin and death have been swallowed up at Calvary. There Christ endured the darkness of God's wrath and quenched the fury of hell's flames. Now through faith the oppressed are released and Satan's captives set free. So lift up your tear-filled eyes and fix them on Jesus.

Though the weeping of repentance endures for a night, the joy of salvation comes in the morning. 'Blessed are the poor in spirit for theirs is the kingdom of heaven. Blessed are those who mourn, for they will be comforted' (Matthew 5:3-4). So do not grieve like those who have no hope, but wet the Saviours's feet with your tears and your many sins will be forgiven.

About the ninth hour Jesus cried out in a loud voice, 'Eloi, Eloi, lama sabachthani?' — which means, 'My God, my God, why have you forsaken me?'

When some of those standing there heard this, they said, 'He's calling Elijah.' (Matthew 27:46-47).

And at the ninth hour Jesus cried out in a loud voice, 'Eloi, Eloi, lama sabachthani?' — which means, 'My God, my God, why have you forsaken me?'

When some of those standing near heard this, they said, 'Listen, he's calling Elijah.' (Mark 15:34-35).

14.
'My God, my God, why have you Forsaken me?'

During the hours of darkness, when 'God made him who had no sin to be sin for us' (2 Corinthians 5:21), the watching crowd was probably hushed in terror and suspense. The mysterious night was beyond their understanding. Its silent menace unanswerable. It was at the end of this dark stillness (3pm our time), in which Christ had endured the full force of God's wrath, that he uttered the fourth word from the cross. 'About the ninth hour Jesus cried out in a loud voice, "Eloi, Eloi, lama sabachthani?" — which means, "My God, my God, why have you forsaken me?"' (Matthew 27:46). These words are taken from Psalm 22 where the sufferings of the Messiah are foretold.

Some commentators, understandably, are reluctant to inquire into the meaning of these words. They say only that they express the extremest bitterness of Christ's bitter cup. Such is the force of these words that it is only with deep reverence and fear that we examine them. We are treading on holy ground and stepping beyond the veil into the mysteries of the cross that are outside human comprehension. We must therefore pray that God will open our minds to grasp what lies before us, giving us grace to see into the heart of our Saviour and to know more fully the exhaustless depths of his suffering and love. We freely acknowledge that the explanation given below falls far short of the reality of Christ's experience.

We must say at the start that Christ did not cry out to complain, but to express the intenseness of the inner sorrow of his soul and the burden of the guilt he bore at the judgment seat of his Father. So dreadful was the curse of the law and the isolation of the cross; so terrible the bitterness of divine wrath and the conflict within his own breast; so abhorrent the iniquity laid on him that 'he felt himself to be in some measure estranged from his Father' (Calvin). There was no sensible consolation to uphold him, no perceivable assistance from heaven. It was as if his own Father opposed him. The horror that tossed him, the wrath that crushed him, the sense of abandonment — all these moved him to cry out. Who else could have borne the 'accumulated sin of the world, from the disobedience of Eden down to the last intention of sin that shall be disturbed by the archangel's trumpet? They all rested upon one human soul, to whom the faintest shadow of sin was intolerable' (Miles). No other! Only the Christ of God could bear what would have swallowed up a hundred times all the men in the world. He alone withstood the terrors of all that was necessary to pay the price for our salvation.

This exclamation, which unveils the agony of Christ's soul, also heralds his faithfulness to and dependence on God. Although his agonies at this point were equivalent to our eternal destruction, he did not at any time turn away from his Father in heaven. He still cried, 'My God, my God'. In the moment of utter desolation, when his spirit plunged to the depths of despair, he called out to the one he loved and trusted. 'During this fearful torture his faith remained uninjured so that, while he complained of being forsaken, he still relied on the aid of God as at hand' (Calvin). Despite the inner turmoil he rested firmly on his Father. He looked heavenward for the succour and strength he needed. It was, in a sense, Gethsemane all over again, where, being overwhelmed with sorrow to the point of death and with his sweat falling to the ground like drops of blood, he prayed, 'Not my will, but yours be done' (Luke 22:42).

There is never any justification for us to forsake God. Often the road of faith is marked with dangers and our hearts are weighed down by trials. Sometimes, like Christ, we are shattered by a sense of divine abandonment. At such times we must look heavenward and petition him who is able to work all things for our good. Our troubles should drive us nearer to God, not away from him. They should motivate us to search more fervently for the Lord, knowing that the search for God is never in vain.

Nor do these words mean that God stopped loving his Son. It was not a withholding of affection or a withdrawing of sustaining strength that made Christ cry out. God cannot reject his Son, or his children, in that way. Our world may be falling apart and the most tragic and unforeseen circumstances darkening the light of God's tender care, yet such distresses should never persuade us that God has blotted out his love for us. The sun is often covered by dark clouds, but it still shines brightly behind them. So God's love is at times shrouded by many trials, but it remains as real and as deep as ever.

There are times when we groan in anguish of heart and imagine that we walk through the valley of the shadow of death without our Father's care. We look up but the heavens are closed. We plead through our tears but the face of God is hidden. There is no hope, or so it seems, of the Lord, who tramples the ancient serpent underfoot, hurrying to our aid. We sigh with David, 'How long, O LORD? Will you forget me for ever? How long will you hide your face from me?' (Psalm 13:1). It is as if we have been cast aside by omnipotent love. But thank God, this sense of abandonment is only momentary! There is always hope for the embattled Christian and relief for an aching heart. The trial may appear to us to last for ever, but when the time is right and its purpose accomplished, God draws near and lifts us up. 'And the God of all grace, who called you to his eternal glory in Christ, after you have suffered a little while, will himself restore you and make you strong, firm and steadfast' (1 Peter 5:10). Through the darkness the light of God shines. Through the tears we see his face.

These desertions, though only temporary, are often experienced by the children of God and, if used aright, secure great benefit to the soul. On the one hand they test and strengthen our faith, if we hold on to the promises of God, and achieve for us an eternal glory that far outweighs them all. A faith that is tossed to and fro by inward conflicts of alienation from God is 'proved genuine' (1 Peter 1:7) by the shaking. It is stronger after the trial than before. A tree that is blown by the wind digs its roots further into the ground. So our faith when it is rocked by the storms of life grips more firmly onto its author and perfecter.

On the other hand, it is during seasons of abandonment that our proud hearts are brought low and our stubborn wills softened for the Master's use. It is so easy to take the credit for success and to boast about self-made prosperity. Almost without realising it we imitate the arrogance of King Nebuchadnezzar who said, 'Is not this the great Babylon I have built as the royal residence, by my mighty power and for the glory of my majesty?' (Daniel 4:30). It was only after he was deposed from his royal throne and stripped of his glory that he acknowledged that 'the Most High God is sovereign over the kingdoms of men and sets over them anyone he wishes' (Daniel 5:21). All too often it is only when God withdraws his sensible presence, and thereby exposes our inadequacies and deficiencies, that we humble ourselves under his mighty hand and admit that apart from him 'we can do nothing' (John 15:5). Abandonments help us to think of ourselves with sober judgment. They motivate us to yield our wills to his Word.

Desertions also increase our desire for God. We pant for him as the thirsty deer pants for streams of water: 'My soul thirsts for God, for the living God. When can I go and meet with God?' (Psalm 42:2). Hunger makes a man long even for the food he would normally detest. An imprisoned soul dreams of the freedom he once enjoyed and vows never again to misuse it. Similarly, a sense of estrangement from God, moves our hearts to yearn for his sweet presence and to determine to live more for his glory. We are like the beloved in the Song of Songs who searched all night for her lover. 'Absence makes the heart grow fonder' is a common proverb and one that is often experienced by the child of God who feels cut off from the 'Father of heavenly lights' (James 1:17). When the rays of God's presence finally break through the clouds, and times of refreshing come, the sense of joy is almost overwhelming. A man whose body is racked with pain cannot contain his delight when deliverance arrives. After the crippled beggar had been healed by Peter he went into the temple courts 'walking and jumping, and praising God' (Acts 3:8). How sweet is the taste of water to a thirsty soul! So satisfying is the nearness of God after a period of dryness, that it is almost worth wandering the barren heights and treading on the parched ground in order to experience the contrast of God's intimate presence.

When some of those standing near heard Christ's cry, they said, 'Listen, he's calling Elijah' (Mark 15:35). Some commentators think that the words of Jesus awakened the consciences of the Jews, who seriously thought that Elijah was about to appear to usher in the day of judgment. Admittedly the Jews were extremely superstitious, and ready to believe almost anything, especially after three hours of supernatural darkness. It is however a misinterpretation to say that their response to the words of Jesus was to expect a sudden Messianic appearance. Nor are we convinced by those who say that the Jews either misheard or misunderstood what Jesus said. In the first place Jesus 'cried out in a loud voice' (Mark 15:34), making his words clearly audible. In the second place, most of the Jews understood both the Hebrew and Aramaic languages; and thirdly, the majority were familiar with Psalm 22 and its meaning. Another implausible explanation is that the reply was spoken, not by the Jews, but by the soldiers. This is improbable because the soldiers were neither conversant with the language of Jesus, nor acquainted with Old Testament prophecy.

We are, though, in full accord with those critics who say it was 'a blasphemous Jewish joke, by an awkward and godless pun upon Eloi' (Meyer). The watching Jews, who could not bear to hear Jesus address God, twisted his words so that he called upon the prophet Elijah and not his own Father. To them it was inconceivable, even laughable, that a 'false' Messiah should implore heaven for help. They ridiculed the very thought, so much so that they never actually answered his cry of abandonment. No doubt they could have presented Christ with endless reasons as to why God had forsaken him, but for them that was secondary. Their most pressing need was to pervert his prayer, and to spread the rumour that he cried to a man and not to God. Even to his final breath, the enemies of God made fun of his Son, trying to discredit all he said and did.

Jesus made no reply to these accusations. His soul was focused on higher things. His thoughts were on eternal issues. He was looking to heaven from where his deliverance would come. 'I lift up my eyes to the hills — where does my help come from? My help comes from the LORD, the Maker of heaven and earth' (Psalm 121:1-2). When the day of evil comes, let us without delay lift our heads to the King of glory and set our hearts on things above, where Christ our rock is seated. He is our fortress and his walls cannot be breached by all the forces of hell. Under his wing the vulnerable find shelter. In his presence the weak are made strong. His faithfulness is our shield and rampart. ' "Because he loves me," says the Lord, "I will rescue him; I will protect him, for he acknowledges my name. He will call upon me, and I will answer him; I will be with him in trouble, I will deliver him and honour him. With long life will I satisfy him and show him my salvation" ' (Psalm 91:14-16).

Immediately one of them ran and got a sponge. He filled it with wine-vinegar, put it on a stick, and offered it to Jesus to drink. But the rest said, 'Leave him alone. Let's see if Elijah comes to save him.' (Matthew 27:48-49).

One man ran, filled a sponge with wine-vinegar, put it on a stick, and offered it to Jesus to drink. 'Leave him alone now. Let's see if Elijah comes to take him down,' he said. (Mark 15:36).

Later, knowing that all was now completed, and so that the Scripture would be fulfilled, Jesus said, 'I am thirsty.' A jar of wine-vinegar was there, so they soaked a sponge in it, put the sponge on a stalk of the hyssop plant, and lifted it to Jesus' lips. (John 19:28-29).

15.
'I am Thirsty'

As the taunts about Elijah resounded in his ears, 'knowing that all was now completed, and so that the Scripture would be fulfilled, Jesus said, "I am thirsty"' (John 19:28). This is his fifth word from the cross and it immediately followed his cry of abandonment. The darkness had dissipated and the heat of the sun again scorched his brow. The debt for sin, outstanding for so long, had finally been paid and eternal salvation earned for his people. He had endured the wrath of God for the sake of the elect and obeyed his Father to the point of death — 'even death on a cross!' (Philippians 2:8). 'All was now completed.'

'Hallelujah! Salvation and glory and power belong to our God' (Revelation 19:1). What is impossible for us, Christ has accomplished. He died that we might live. He was crushed by God's wrath that we might enjoy his mercy, and pierced by the torments of hell that we might rejoice in heaven. He was made a little lower than the angels, 'now crowned with glory and honour because he suffered death so that by the grace of God he might taste death for everyone' (Hebrews 2:9). Hallelujah! Christ has completed his Father's work. There is nothing left for us to do but to take hold of the fruit of that work, to rejoice in him for ever, and to spend ourselves for his glory, knowing that whoever believes in him 'will live, even though he dies' (John 11:25).

Jesus knew that relief would not arrive until God's will had been accomplished. But as soon as the final blow had been struck and with the trumpet of triumph about to sound, he said, 'I am thirsty'. Lange comments that 'with the presentiment of victory, his thirst makes itself felt. And he, being no legal ascetic, nor despising a service rendered by the hand of sinners, requests and partakes of the last, sorry refreshment.' The words of Christ fulfilled Psalm 22:15. This whole Psalm has been described as the gospel according to David, so many are the allusions and references, direct and indirect, to the passion, death, resurrection and glory of Christ. In verse fifteen David, speaking as a type of the Messiah, says, 'My strength is dried up like a potsherd, and my tongue sticks to the roof of my mouth; you lay me in the dust of death.' One of the tortures of crucifixion was an excruciating thirst.

The three words 'I am thirsty' evidence the depth of Christ's suffering, which, for six long hours, had been endured in a calm and controlled manner. They look behind the scenes, as it were, and touch on the severity of the conflict that raged within his soul — a conflict that words alone cannot describe with sufficient force. It was a conflict he had battled through alone, without the sensible presence of his Father, without the angel that had strengthened him at Gethsemane, without the comfort and support of his family or friends, who could only watch from a distance. It was a secret struggle with which no one could properly relate or sympathise. For two thousand years men and women have striven in vain to understand its intensity.

These three words also bear witness to his humanity. The one through whom all things were made shared in our flesh and blood with all its frailties. He became 'like his brothers in every way' in order to become 'a merciful and faithful high priest in service to God' and to 'make atonement for the sins of the people' (Hebrews 2:17). He was 'born of a woman, born under law' (Galatians 4:4) so as to redeem those who all their lives had been suffering under the demands and condemnation of the law. He was tempted in every way, just as we are — 'yet was without sin' (Hebrews 4:15). He was hungry in the wilderness after forty days and nights of fasting. He was weary as the storm raged on the Sea of Galilee. He was overwhelmed with sorrow to the point of death in the garden of Gethsemane. He was thirsty — oh yes, he was thirsty! — thirsty for our salvation, thirsty to finish his Father's work, thirsty as he bore our punishment on the cross at Calvary. He who is the fountain of living water endured the burning thirst of hell. As a result all who believe in him will never have to plead with Father Abraham to send 'Lazarus to dip the tip of his finger in water to cool my tongue, because I am in agony in this fire' (Luke 16:24).

Upon hearing Christ call out, one of the soldiers, probably acting on the orders of the centurion and with the help of others, soaked a sponge in a jar of wine vinegar that was there. He put it 'on a stalk of the hyssop plant, and lifted it to Jesus' lips' (John 19:29). Some conjecture that it was not a soldier but one of the watching friends of Jesus who offered him the wine vinegar to drink. They quote Mark who simply says it was a 'man' (15:36). This is unlikely though because only the soldiers would have been permitted to interfere with Jesus. On this ground most believe it was one of the men who had crucified Jesus and then cast lots for his clothing.

Another question that needs to be addressed is: Was it an act of genuine sympathy for Christ or just another cruel joke? The older critics seem to take the latter view. They argue that Jesus would have found the wine-vinegar bitter and nauseous, and totally unsuitable for quenching thirst. If anything, they say, it would have increased his discomfort. In support of this view it must not be forgotten that these same soldiers had earlier mocked Christ by sarcastically challenging him to save himself if he was the king of the Jews (Luke 23:36-37). The majority of modern commentators, who rightly distinguish this episode from Mark 15:23 (cf Matthew 27:34) where Jesus was offered 'wine mixed with myrrh, but he did not take it', say that the soldiers were acting out of compassion for Christ. The soldiers honestly wanted to relieve his parched lips and throat. They base their opinion on the 'wine-vinegar', which, they say, would not have been bitter and nauseous to the taste, because it was the same sour and diluted wine that the soldiers drank with their midday meal.

If the soldiers were acting kindly to Christ, what had changed them from callous mockers into genuine sympathisers? Since their initial jesting, some six hours earlier, these men had heard the gracious words of Christ to the dying thief, the instructions of love to his mother and John, and the anguished cry to his Father. They had witnessed the calm and dignified way in which he had suffered, and experienced the three hours of supernatural darkness. All this may have softened their hearts, thus moving them to extend a hand of mercy to our Lord.

Even the most hardened individuals are capable of acts of kindness, especially to their own kind or to those in dire need. Tax collectors love those who love them and even pagans greet their brothers. An embittered man who is violently opposed to authority is capable of expressing the most touching tenderness to his own son. There are many who would not lift a finger to help their healthy neighbour, but who are quite prepared to minister to the sick. Some people would not walk across the road to befriend the rich, but they would travel many miles in aid of the poor.

We are complex and often contradictory beings. Out of the same mouth come praise and cursing. From the same heart proceed acts of callousness and of the most moving philanthropy. One minute we sympathise with our troubled friend and wholeheartedly condemn his persecutors. The next we fly into a rage when he falsely accuses us of supporting their wrongdoing. With force we publicly uphold Biblical morals before our peers and then commit adultery in the privacy of our hearts. We listen when one man speaks and gain from his instruction. When another stands, perhaps because of his shabby appearance, we ignore him. On Monday we forgive our neighbour his debts. On Tuesday we bang on his door and demand payment in full. With care we try and remove the speck in our brother's eye, while excusing the plank in our own. We vehemently denounce the sins of the world while practising many of them in secret. We shout 'Amen!' as the preacher roars out threats against the wicked, but as soon as we are out of earshot of the sermon we walk hand in hand with them to their dens of iniquity.

As Christians these things should not be. 'Can both fresh water and salt water flow from the same spring? Can a fig-tree bear olives, or a grape-vine bear figs?' (James 3:11-12). Should a child of God, who is heaven bound, act as a minion of Satan, whose eternal abode is in hell? Are we as the light of the world expected to imitate the fruitless deeds of darkness? These very suggestions are an abomination! We are to be blameless and pure, 'without fault in a crooked and depraved generation' (Philippians 2:15). We are to adorn ourselves with garments that are unsoiled by the filth of this world. An unholy Christian is an absurdity. With his actions he denies the truth he claims to uphold and condemns as a sham the faith he professes. 'Faith by itself, if it is not accompanied by action, is dead' (James 2:17). It is a corpse that has an appearance of being alive but is void of the breath of life. A ventriloquist can make his dummy speak, or so it seems, but that dummy is without the smallest spark of life in its wooden body. So is the man who makes great boasts about his faith but does not partner it with action. He is a spiritual dummy, lifeless and moved by the hand of deceit.

We must not deceive ourselves into believing that just because we agree with our church's statement of faith all is well with our soul. What is our life like? Does it conform to the teachings of the Bible? Are we producing good fruit? Is the testimony of our hearts the same as the testimony of our lips? We must test ourselves to see if we are in the faith. It is a horrifying delusion to think we are treading the golden path to heaven when actually we are sliding towards the mouth of hell.

When the soldiers offered the wine-vinegar to Jesus, they were inadvertently fulfilling Psalm 69:21b. Charles Hodge, a leading American theologian of the last century, says that the whole Psalm is 'so frequently quoted and applied to Christ in the New Testament, that it must be considered as directly prophetical.' (The first half of verse 21 was fulfilled by the soldiers before the crucifixion when they offered Jesus 'wine mixed with myrrh' [Mark 15:23], which he refused to drink.) The wine soaked sponge was placed 'on a stalk of the hyssop plant'. This was sturdy enough to hold a wet sponge and long enough to reach Jesus, who was not very high off the ground. The plant may have been the wild marjoram, an aromatic herb, the fresh or dried leaves of which are used as a flavouring in cookery. Jesus would have sucked the moisture from the sponge and, to some extent, relieved his thirst. Some think that this refreshment gave him enough strength to utter his last two words from the cross.

Hyssop is a well-known Biblical plant. It was used by the Jews for ritual sprinklings and by their forefathers in Egypt to put the blood of the passover lamb on the top and on both sides of the door-frame, thus saving them from the 'destroyer' (Exodus 12:22-23). David in Psalm 51:7 says, 'Cleanse me with hyssop, and I shall be clean.' It is everywhere used in connection with cleansing and deliverance. How fitting then, that the Pioneer of our salvation, at the moment of victory, should have a sponge on a hyssop plant pressed to his lips. It reminds us that we are no longer sprinkled with the blood of animals, for 'it is impossible for the blood of bulls and goats to take away sins' (Hebrews 10:4), 'but with the precious blood of Christ, a lamb without blemish or defect' (1 Peter 1:19). His death cleanses our guilty consciences and purifies us from every sin.

As the soldier was lifting the sponge to Jesus, others near the cross tried to stop him, 'Leave him alone. Let's see if Elijah comes to save him' (Matthew 27:49). With deep sarcasm they pretended that Elijah, the Messiah's forerunner, had heard his cry and was considering whether or not to answer it. To them the whole thing was nothing but a joke. It was a chance to make sport of a dying man and to accuse Jesus of being forsaken by both God and men.

So Jesus, amid the snarls of angry men, reached the brink of death. The night of wrath was nearly over. A few moments more and death would be his deliverer. Today, for some who look back to the cross, the death of Christ was the beginning of a new age in which righteousness and peace are preached the world over for the praise of the glory of God. For others, blinded by prejudice and malice, it was just another day, much like any other. To some the man who cried 'I am thirsty' is 'the Saviour of all men' (1 Timothy 4:10) who quenches thirsty souls with the water of life. To others Jesus was just another man, no different from the next. To the redeemed the cross of Christ is the fragrance of life, to the condemned it is the stench of death.

And when Jesus had cried out again in a loud voice, he gave up his spirit. (Matthew 27:50).

With a loud cry, Jesus breathed his last. (Mark 15:37).

Jesus called out with a loud voice, 'Father, into your hands I commit my spirit.' When he had said this, he breathed his last. (Luke 23:46).

When he had received the drink, Jesus said, 'It is finished.' With that, he bowed his head and gave up his spirit. (John 19:30).

16.
'It is Finished'

The ultimate battle had been fought and won, and the arms of victory laid down. The dregs from the cup filled with the wine of God's wrath had been swallowed and the full price of redemption paid. The nakedness of death was about to be exchanged for the conqueror's robe, and the crown of thorns, so crudely tangled together by callous men, was soon to be replaced by the crown of eternal glory; for the storm that had raged so violently was over and peace reigned.

After Jesus had received the reviving refreshment from the wine-vinegar he again lifted his voice and said, 'It is finished.' In the original this statement is only one word. It is the briefest yet fullest word spoken by Christ from the cross. Krummacher, a nineteenth century German Reformed pastor and writer, says it is 'the greatest and most momentous word that was ever spoken upon earth since the beginning of the world.' Its meaning is so profound that we can only begin to appreciate its richness and to fathom its depths. It is a word of truth that seals the work of Christ and imparts to all who look to him a sure and heavenly hope. It is a word, common throughout the world, yet uttered by the God-Man to herald his victory over sin and Satan. It is simple enough to read, but how glorious and life-changing is its significance to those who embrace its author!

The word 'finished' means consummated or to bring to completion, and it pertains to the whole of salvation. The work of redemption, from beginning to end, is fully, perfectly, eternally accomplished. The justice of God is wholly satisfied and the redemption of sinners guaranteed. The powers and authorities are disarmed. The dominion of sin and death are terminated, and the gates of hell closed for ever to the believer. All is finished. There is nothing wanting. Nothing has been forgotten or left unfulfilled. E.B.Pusey remarks that 'in one human word our Lord gathered into one all that he had willed and wrought and suffered for man's salvation. Finished was the determinate counsel of God. Finished was all that prophecy had foretold and type foreshadowed, and patriarchs and righteous men had longed to see and angels desired to look into. Finished was the work that the Father gave him to do and the deliverance he had wrought in the earth. Finished were all the sufferings that the malice of man and Satan could inflict, and the cup of his Father's wrath. Finished was the transgression and an end made of sin. Finished was the one sacrifice for sin and the mortal life of God made man, the victory over Satan, his rule and our enthralment.'

Yes, Christ has finished the work of salvation, so who can point an accusing finger at God's elect? Who can condemn those whom God has justified through faith? Who has the right to taunt a believer with the cry that God has rejected him because he has failed to keep the law? Thank God we are justified 'by faith in Christ and not by observing the law' (Galatians 2:16). Even if we were faultless in legalistic righteousness and a Pharisee of Pharisees, it would be nothing more than dung as far as salvation is concerned. There is a righteousness from God, apart from law, to all who believe in Christ and his atoning death. It is a perfect righteousness that is neither stained nor revoked by sin — a righteousness that means the believer shall never be punished with everlasting destruction or shut out from the presence of the Lord and from the majesty of his power. If 'we have been justified by his blood, how much more shall we be saved from God's wrath through him!' (Romans 5:9). We have been reconciled to God 'through the death of his Son' (Romans 5:10). We have received the Spirit of sonship by whom we cry 'Abba Father' (Romans 8:15), and since we are sons, God has made us also heirs — 'heirs of God and co-heirs with Christ' (Romans 8:17).

How futile of men and women to regard the finished work of Christ as 'not good enough'! Some try to make up for what they think is lacking by offering good works and penances and religious sacrifices to God on their man-made altars, hoping he will look upon them more favourably. They resort to human effort to 'back up' their faith. They rely on the weak and miserable principles of the world to improve their standing before heaven, observing special days and months and seasons and years, and basing their religion on human commands and teachings, which are all destined to perish. They deny themselves pleasures that are lawful and right and adhere to ascetic practices that have an appearance of wisdom, with their self-imposed worship and harsh treatment of the body, but which lack any value in restraining sensual indulgence — all in a vain attempt to 'complete' what has already been completed.

How terrible it is to consider the work of Christ as unfinished and to imagine that we, by our feeble efforts, might improve on it! Is there anything more insulting to Christ, who bore our sins in his body on the tree, than to behave in such a way that heralds our dissatisfaction with his death and that at the same time expresses confidence in our own works? It is preposterous to think that the actions of hell-deserving sinners are necessary to render complete the Lord of glory's work. Perish the very thought! Instead of boasting about our own righteousness, which is as filthy rags in God's sight, we should humble ourselves and bow before our Saviour. It is through his death that we are redeemed from the curse of the law. We should put away every notion of 'adding' to Christ's work and echo in our hearts the words of hope for men: 'It is finished.'

Knowing that his work was completed 'Jesus called out with a loud voice, "Father, into your hands I commit my spirit" '

(Luke 23:46). His final word from the cross was not the murmur of an exhausted, defeated criminal, or the feeble whisper that exudes from other dying men, but the strong cry of an uninjured soul, whose confidence in God all could plainly hear. It was a 'loud cry' (Mark 15:37) from the conqueror of death, whose life did not ebb away in weakness, but who willingly poured himself out unto death. In strength Christ departed this world of woe. In his first word from the cross Christ called on his Father to forgive his persecutors, 'for they do not know what they are doing' (Luke 23:34). In his last, using the words of Psalm 31:5 and having regained the consciousness of his Father's presence, he called out to the one he loved to receive his spirit. So with serenity and perfect control, and with Scripture on his lips, he entrusted his soul to his Father's safe keeping. He 'came from the Father and entered the world'; he was now 'leaving the world and going back to the Father' (John 16:28). His faith remained unshaken by the trials that had assaulted it and his confidence in divine love was as resolute as it had always been.

It is at the moment of death that faith is often sorely shaken by the accusations of Satan. He fires arrows of doubt and despair into the hearts and minds of departing saints in an attempt to undermine their childlike trust in God. We need not fear, though, for the one who has watched over us throughout our earthly pilgrimage will not forsake us as we breathe our last. He is the faithful guardian of our souls in life and in death. When the final hour tolls, he will equip us to depart cheerfully to be with Christ 'which is better by far' (Philippians 1:23). That is why our Saviour could commit his spirit into his Father's hands with composure and hope. In so doing he committed all the souls who would believe on him in the world into his eternal care. It is the greatest blessing of all to put off the body of death with its weaknesses and pains and frustrations, to lay down our weapons with which we have fought many a bruising battle, and to enter into the glorious presence of God. It is the goal of our faith and the end of the long and often arduous race. Laid up for us there are the treasures of heaven and the crown of righteousness, which the Lord will award 'to all who have longed for his appearing' (2 Timothy 4:8).

So Jesus, looking to the joy that was set before him and welcoming the rest of death, 'bowed his head and gave up his spirit' (John 19:30). After death the head usually flops uncontrollably onto the chest; but with Jesus, before he 'breathed his last' (Mark 15:37), as a final act of dignity and submission, he gently and reverently lowered his head. Up until his dying breath he had held his head steady and unmoved. But when the moment of release came, with perfect control, he 'bowed his head'. The anguish, the torture, the mockery, the wrath of God and even death itself could not extinguish the indwelling authority with which he governed all his words, thoughts and deeds.

When Christ bowed his head he was, in effect, saying to all who would believe on him, 'Stand up and lift your heads, because your redemption is drawing near' (Luke 21:28). Thanks be to Christ — deliverance is at hand! Our brief troubles and momentary tears will soon be exchanged for heaven's lasting peace and eternal joy. The desert of death, visited by us all, will be turned into a pool of life-giving water and our wilderness will blossom. The cross we bear today will be the crown we wear tomorrow, and the insults that come from the world will in that hour be drowned by the Master's voice, 'Well done, good and faithful servant! Come and share your master's happiness!' (Matthew 25:21). And it is all because of Christ who bowed his head in death.

Finally, under no compulsion or reluctance, Christ 'gave up his spirit' (Matthew 27:50). None of the gospel writers say that Christ died, as if to emphasise that his death, which was a real separation of soul and body, was the voluntary act of his own will. No one took his life. He laid it down of his own accord (John 10:17-18), offering himself to God. He died because he wanted to die and not because of the pains of crucifixion. It was an act of free dying by the Lord and Master of death. 'I am the good shepherd. The good shepherd lays down his life for the sheep' (John 10:11). Death could not come until he willed it.

'Forever let us bless God that Christ gave up his spirit, and really died upon the cross before myriads of witnesses. In vain Christ's life and miracles and preaching, if Christ had not at last died for us! We needed not merely a teacher, but an atonement and the death of a substitute. The mightiest transaction that ever took place on earth since the fall of man was accomplished when Jesus gave up his spirit' (Ryle). It bought back what was lost by Adam and restored to us 'the full rights of sons' (Galatians 4:5). The result of Adam's trespass was condemnation and death for all men. The result of Christ's obedience, even to death, was 'justification that brings life to all men' (Romans 5:18). Instead of death, life; instead of condemnation, justification; instead of the many made sinners, the many will be made righteous; instead of sin reigning in death, grace will 'reign through righteousness to bring eternal life through Jesus Christ our Lord' (Romans 5:21).

How then should we live for him? Should we not lay our lives at his feet for him to use as he will? Is it too much for us, when he sends us to the ends of the earth, to go cheerfully and without hesitation? If he presents us with an opportunity to share the good news with our neighbour, are we prepared to take it gratefully? When he speaks, are we in the right frame of mind to sit at his feet and listen? When he asks, 'Whom shall I send? And who will go for us?', is our response, 'Here am I. Send me!' (Isaiah 6:8)? 'Whatever you will, wherever you send, whenever you call, I am ready to obey, Lord' is the Christian attitude.

> Take my life and let it be
> Consecrated, Lord, to thee;
> Take my moments and my days,
> Let them flow in ceaseless praise.

Take my will and make it thine;
It shall be no longer mine:
Take my heart, it is thine own;
It shall be thy royal throne.

Take my love; my Lord, I pour
At thy feet its treasure store:
Take myself and I will be
Ever, only, all for thee.

Frances R Havergal 1836-79

So the sun of righteousness passed into his Father's presence. Never again was he to suffer wrath or to lay down his life as an atonement for sin. The battle was over and the victory won. He sank to rest, 'changing the storm, the tragedy, and the cross by heroism, wondrous words and prayers, into light and glory, deepening into serenity and rest. There was such a nobleness and greatness in the whole we cannot think of it as death. It was but a setting, his life's work crowned' (Thomas). When he appears a second time, it will not be to bear the sins of the world, 'but to bring salvation to those who are waiting for him' (Hebrews 9:28). Until that day, as we cling to the old rugged cross on which the Lord of glory died, 'let us hold unswervingly to the hope we profess, for he who promised is faithful' (Hebrews 10:23). Let us set our hearts and minds on things above, where our Saviour is seated at the right hand of God. And if at times we are tempted to doubt the efficacy of Christ's blood, considering ourselves as too vile to be cleansed or wanting to 'make up' for what was supposedly missing at Calvary, let us remember the words of life that passed from the lips of our dying Substitute: 'It is finished.' There is no more that needs to be done. It is finished once for all evermore.

At that moment the curtain of the temple was torn in two from top to bottom. (Matthew 27:51a).

The curtain of the temple was torn in two from top to bottom. (Mark 15:38).

And the curtain of the temple was torn in two. (Luke 23:45b).

17.
The Torn Curtain

At the moment of Christ's death 'the curtain of the temple was torn in two from top to bottom' (Mark 15:38). This curtain was the inner partition that separated the Holy Place from the Most Holy Place. It was made of cloth and beautifully embroidered with cherubim, looped at either end and suspended by two corners so that the high priest could enter the holy sanctuary by the side of it. Only the high priest was allowed behind the curtain 'and that only once a year, and never without blood, which he offered for himself and for the sins the people had committed in ignorance' (Hebrews 9:7). It was a reminder that the way into the Most Holy Place 'had not yet been disclosed' (Hebrews 9:8).

At about the ninth hour, toward the time of the evening sacrifice, when Caiaphas the high priest was burning incense in front of the curtain and the other priests were busily performing their religious duties in other parts of the temple, the curtain was torn into two pieces and the Most Holy Place opened to view. What a shock for Caiaphas suddenly to see behind the curtain, for him to look into the forbidden room and behold the ark of the covenant! What terror must have gripped the hearts of the bewildered priests, and how quickly they must have fled from the temple in fear of their lives, shouting, 'The curtain is torn! The curtain is torn!' This striking incident probably had a profound effect on some of them. It could have been a reason why, after the day of Pentecost, as the Word of

God spread throughout Jerusalem, 'a large number of priests became obedient to the faith' (Acts 6:7).

It seems to have made no impression on Caiaphas, though. He was the one who had told the Sanhedrin that it was better for them 'that one man die for the people than that the whole nation perish' (John 11:50). Thus he had prophesied, albeit unwittingly, 'that Jesus would die for the Jewish nation' as well as the 'scattered children of God, to bring them together and make them one' (John 11:51-52). At Christ's trial he had asked Jesus, 'Are you the Christ, the Son of the Blessed One?' (Mark 14:61). When Jesus replied 'I am', and described his position at the 'right hand of the Mighty One' and his coming again in judgment (Mark 14:62), Caiaphas 'tore his clothes' and accused Jesus of blasphemy (Mark 14:63). At the time of our Lord's death, as Caiaphas stood ministering in the temple, he saw with his own eyes the holy curtain ripped in two, yet he remained unmoved. There is no hint that he understood its significance. There is no mention of him tearing his clothes in horror, no suggestion that he regarded it as an act of God. Probably, like so many have tried to do, he explained it away as a freak accident, dismissing its timing as coincidental.

Unless God removes the veil that blinds our hearts to the truth as it is in Christ, nothing we do or see or experience will make us believe. The darkness of Calvary could overshadow us, and the tombs of our fathers break open; the idols we worship could fall to the ground and break into many pieces, just as Dagon was thrown down before the ark of the Lord; but if God does not impart to us the gift of repentance and faith, our hearts will remain firmly entrenched in the ways of this world. Salvation is God's work of grace from beginning to end. It is not based on a decision we made years ago, or on a religious experience we had when we were a child. It is not founded on our position in the church, or on the good works we perform. No! It is God who opens the eyes of the blind and raises to life those who are dead in transgressions and sins.

On the other hand, in case we are tempted to use the sovereignty of God as an excuse for impenitence, we need to understand that it is only when we turn to the Lord that 'the veil is taken away' (2 Corinthians 3:16). Our responsibility is to 'repent and believe the good news' (Mark 1:15). We are not asked to save ourselves from sin and its consequences, but we are commanded to 'repent and turn to God' and to prove our repentance by our deeds (Acts 26:20). It is a lie of Satan that says, because we cannot earn salvation, we must not seek it; or, because we cannot overcome sin in our own strength, we must never try to forsake it. Again and again the Scriptures bid us to 'seek the Lord while he may be found' and to 'call on him while he is near. Let the wicked forsake his way and the evil man his thoughts. Let him turn to the Lord, and he will have mercy on him, and to our God, for he will freely pardon' (Isaiah 55:6-7). We cannot save ourselves, but we must, with humble hearts and contrite spirits, run to the Saviour who can.

Some, in a vain attempt to exclude the intervention of God, say the curtain was torn because of natural wear and tear. If that was the case, it would have been gradually torn from bottom to top over a long period of time and shown other signs of deterioration. According to the testimony of Jewish scholars the curtain was renewed whenever necessary and always before it reached a poor state of repair. Others, who at least find their reason in the Bible, think the tear was caused by the earthquake. Only Matthew mentions the earthquake, which he says occurred after the curtain was torn. It was as if the earth shook because the curtain was torn, not vice versa. But even if we allow for an inaccuracy in Matthew's chronology, it is extremely fanciful to teach that an earthquake tore the curtain from top to bottom without damaging the rest of the temple. Surely large cracks would have appeared in the walls and roof from the shaking. Perhaps part of the temple would have collapsed.

From the Gospel texts and from other parts of the New Testament it is apparent that the tearing of the curtain was a highly significant act of God. The curtain represented a barrier between God and man, a sign of exclusion that read 'Keep out!' It showed that the ceremonial law, with its sacrifices for sins that were repeated year after year, only secured an imperfect reconciliation between God and his people. It could never 'make perfect those who draw near to worship' (Hebrews 10:1). If those sacrifices had satisfied the justice of God, then the 'worshippers would have been cleansed once for all, and would no longer have felt guilty for their sins', or continued to offer sacrifices (Hebrews 10:2). As it was, those sacrifices, which could only make the guilty outwardly clean, were an 'annual reminder of sins, because it is impossible for the blood of bulls and goats to take away sins' (Hebrews 10:3-4). The curtain in the temple told everyone that something was not right with their standing before God.

When God tore the curtain it was as if he was tearing the ceremonial law in two and breaking down the barrier that had existed between God and man since the fall of Adam. He was declaring that Christ's death had not only done away with sin and obtained eternal redemption, but had fulfilled and accomplished all the Levitical rites and figures, and rendered obsolete the typical offerings and priestly mediation. Atonement was complete. Sins were washed away, 'and where these have been forgiven, there is no longer any sacrifice for sin' (Hebrews 10:18). In short, God was destroying the temple and abolishing the Jewish dispensation.

This means that 'we have confidence to enter the Most Holy Place by the blood of Jesus, by a new and living way opened for us through the curtain', that is, Christ's body (Hebrews 10:19-20). There is no need for us to be like Moses, who at the sight of God's glory said, 'I am trembling with fear' (Hebrews 12:21). There is no need for us to beg God not to speak to us as the Israelites did, 'because they could not bear what was commanded' (Hebrews 12:20). On the contrary, we are told that through faith in Christ 'we may approach God with freedom and confidence' (Ephesians 3:12). We should expect to 'receive mercy and find grace to help us in our time of need' (Hebrews 4:16). Every obstruction has been removed. Not even sin is a barrier any more. Calvin says that the rending of the veil 'was, in some respects, an opening of heaven, that God may now invite the members of his Son to approach him with familiarity.' The way is open. God and man have been reconciled 'by Christ's physical body through death' (Colossians 1:22). The enmity that alienated us has been dealt with. The written code with its regulations that opposed us has been nailed to the cross.

Even those who were once far away from God, 'excluded from citizenship in Israel and foreigners to the covenants of promise' (Ephesians 2:12), have been brought near to God through the blood of Christ. People from every tribe and nation have been purchased for God by his death. Christ is not only the Saviour of the Jews, but also 'a light for revelation to the Gentiles' (Luke 2:32). His salvation is world-embracing. It is a gospel for all mankind. The message that resounds from the cross is that there is free access into God's presence for 'whoever believes' in Christ (John 3:16). 'Whoever is thirsty, let him come; and whoever wishes, let him take the free gift of the water of life' (Revelation 22:17). Nationality, language, genealogy are no longer barriers — Christ died for the world.

Once we have entered the heavenly sanctuary, God's promise to us is: 'Never will I leave you; never will I forsake you' (Hebrews 13:5). Even when we are not conscious of his presence, we know by faith that he still abides with us. God is not a man that he should one day receive us as friends and the next treat us as strangers. He is faithful to the covenant he has established with us. He will not reject those who have come to him through the death of his Son.

When the curtain was torn the need for a high priest in the order of Aaron to represent us before God was set aside. These high priests were selected from among men and were subject to the weaknesses of sin and death, which prevented them from continuing in office. Christ, however, was 'designated by God to be a high priest in the order of Melchizedek' (Hebrews 5:10). He became a priest, not on the basis of regulation as to his ancestry, 'but on the basis of the power of an indestructible life' (Hebrews 7:16). He is therefore 'able to save completely those who come to God through him, because he always lives to intercede for them' (Hebrews 7:25). For that reason we do not need another priest to represent us before God. There is 'one mediator between God and men, the man Christ Jesus' (1 Timothy 2:5). We approach God only through him. That is why it is a denial of Christ's high priestly office, and indeed his work on the cross, to 'confess' our sins to another intermediary, hoping to obtain absolution. To receive an ecclesiastical declaration of forgiveness of sins may pacify our consciences for awhile, but it does not pacify God. The glorious truth of the gospel is that sinners can draw near to God, not through other sinners, but through the Son, 'who has been made perfect for ever' (Hebrews 7:28).

A further benefit of Christ's death to which the torn curtain points is that the dividing wall of hostility between Jew and Gentile has been broken down. Christ, through his death, 'abolished the law in all its forms as a rule of justification. Thus he opened one new way of access to God common to Jews and Gentiles' (Hodge). He reconciled both to God through the cross, and created in himself one new man out of the two, thus making peace. In this new unity the old distinctions of race, religion, culture and social standing cease to count. What matters is Christ, 'our common centre, our standard of reference and fount of honour. He is the sum of all we acknowledge and desire. He is the common life and soul of his people, the substance of all we experience and possess as

Christians' (Findlay). To all who believe, whatever their background, 'Christ is all, and is in all' (Colossians 3:11).

In view of the fact that God's purpose was to create one new man out of the two and to join them together to become 'a holy temple in the Lord' (Ephesians 2:21), we could almost say, although it is not strictly accurate in a theological sense, that when the curtain was torn, it was not so much to let us into the Most Holy Place, as to let God out, so that he could live in the hearts of his people. We are now 'God's temple' (1 Corinthians 6:16), built into a spiritual house 'in which God lives by his Spirit' (Ephesians 2:22). God has turned his back on the temple in Jerusalem in order to dwell more intimately with his children, who 'are the temple of the living God. As God has said, "I will live with them and walk among them, and I will be their God, and they will be my people" ' (2 Corinthians 6:16).

Finally the rent veil discloses that through Christ's death the way to heaven stands open. The road ahead, though narrow and with few pilgrims travelling on it, is clear. It is marked out for us by the Spirit of God, who lives in our hearts. He is 'a deposit guaranteeing our inheritance until the redemption of those who are God's possession' (Ephesians 1:14). He is our hope of future glory. Instead of having to face the awful consequences of sin, all who have been bought with the blood of God, freely enter the small gate that leads to life. Paradise is on our horizon. The holy city, 'whose architect and builder is God' (Hebrews 11:10), where thousands upon thousands of angels join together in joyful assembly and where the spirits of righteous men are made perfect, is in sight. It is just the other side of death. To breathe our last on earth is to breathe our first in heaven. To wave a final goodbye to our friends in this world is to enter the hallowed courts of the Lamb of God, before whom a great multitude stand and worship.

This is our hope, which no man can deny us nor demon spoil. It is a living hope that is stored up for us in heaven and realised at the moment of death. If at present we are suffering many trials and sore temptations, we must not despair, 'for our light and momentary troubles are achieving for us an eternal glory that far outweighs them all' (2 Corinthians 4:17). Let us turn our eyes away from the grief and pain that surround us, for they are transient, to the eternal realities of heaven, which are clearly visible through the eye of faith. It is not a cessation of sorrow that relieves an aching heart, but a vision of the paradise of God. When we lift our thoughts toward the goal of our faith, we become like Christ, who for the joy of redeeming his people endured the cross, scorning its shame. In all the fiery afflictions of life that we pass through, we must 'consider him who endured such opposition from sinful men, so that we will not grow weary and lose heart' (Hebrews 12:3).

The earth shook and the rocks split. The tombs broke open and the bodies of many holy people who had died were raised to life. They came out of the tombs, and after Jesus' resurrection they went into the holy city and appeared to many people. (Matthew 27:51b-53).

18.
The Earthquake and
the Open Tombs

Matthew, who was present in Jerusalem at the time of Christ's death and therefore qualified to explain many of the events that occurred at Calvary, is the only Gospel writer to mention the earthquake. From what he says about the timing and extent of the earthquake it is apparent that the Lord of heaven and earth, who holds the whole world in his hands and before whom the nations tremble, was shaking Jerusalem and its vicinity in order to display his wrath at the crucifixion of Christ.

It was as if God was rocking the holy city backwards and forwards so as to shake its citizens out of the sleep of death and to alert them to their impending judgment. It was a foretelling of those days when 'your enemies will build an embankment against you and encircle you and hem you in on every side. They will dash you to the ground, you and the children within your walls. They will not leave one stone on another, because you did not recognise the time of God's coming to you' (Luke 19:43-44). In those days the people of Jerusalem will be thrown down without mercy, for they disowned the Holy and Righteous One and spurned the salvation of God. They refused to humble themselves before the Saviour of Israel, dismissing Christ, the long-awaited Messiah, as a deceiver and a blasphemer.

Today there are many imitators of the Jews, men and women who turn away from the Christ of the Bible, which depicts the Lord of glory as crucified in weakness yet raised to life by the power of God. In his place they look to other man-made messiahs who pander to their evil desires and say what their itching ears want to hear. These so-called saviours promise their disciples the crown of paradise without the cross of suffering, forgiveness without sacrifice, and life without death. They encourage the gratification of the flesh instead of a walk of holiness and a life of obedience to God's commandments. By mouthing 'empty, boastful words and, by appealing to the lustful desires of sinful human nature, they entice people who are just escaping from those who live in error. They promise them freedom, while they themselves are slaves of depravity' (2 Peter 2:18-19). One moment they accuse Christ of blasphemy, the next they set themselves up in his place. They are 'springs without water and mists driven by a storm' (2 Peter 2:17), for whom blackest darkness has been reserved for ever.

Calvary's earthquake was a manifestation of heaven's power that resembled the days of the exodus when God descended on Mount Sinai in fire and smoke and 'the whole mountain trembled violently' (Exodus 19:18). It was not a minor rumble or a slight tremor, as some conjecture, but a severe shaking. Matthew recalls that 'the earth shook and the rocks split' (27:51) and, as a result, the tombs of many holy people 'broke open' (27:52). It would not be an exaggeration to say that the foundations of the holy city began to crack and crumble as they were rocked to and fro. Schaff, the nineteenth century church historian, reports that 'travellers still point us to extraordinary rents and fissures in the rocks near the supposed or real spot of the crucifixion, as the effects of this earthquake.'

Just as God shook the earth at the time of Christ's death, breaking rocks into pieces and opening tombs, so he is able to break open the hardest heart and subdue, with a word of rebuke, all his foes. Enormous difficulties, which appear as immovable mountains to the minds of men, crumble into dust as he approaches. Before him the walls of Jericho collapsed. With his strength the promised land was conquered. At his command the Red Sea parted so that the Israelites could escape from the Egyptian army. Are we facing a crisis of mammoth proportions, the dangers of which seem insurmountable to us? Stand back, for when God moves on our behalf the age-old hills are trodden down and a way is made through the waters. With God on our side the pursuing enemy is hurled into the deep and what is afflicting us is crushed beneath his feet.

Since that day the gospel of Jesus Christ has rocked empires and governments, shattered the arm of the mighty and broken into pieces the hearts of men. It has overthrown the ruler of the kingdom of the air and released his captives into the glorious freedom of the children of God. It has turned whole nations from the ignorant worship of idols to the adoration of the living and holy God, and transformed violent blasphemers like Paul into men who resolve to know nothing 'except Jesus Christ and him crucified' (1 Corinthians 2:2). It has challenged the morality and ideologies of this world and condemned the futility of man's godless wisdom. It has been, in every sense, a spiritual earthquake that has forcefully shaken the foundations on which our lives are built.

During the earthquake 'the tombs broke open and the bodies of many holy people who had died were raised to life. They came out of the tombs, and after Jesus' resurrection they went into the holy city and appeared to many people' (Matthew 27:52-53). 'The Jewish sepulchres were natural or artificial excavations in rocks. The entrances were closed by doors or large stones. Hence it may be supposed that, beside the rending of rocks, the stone doors of the graves were removed by the force of the earthquake' (Schaff). It may also be supposed that God broke open the tombs, without the aid of the earthquake, as a distinct act of his power.

Some have perverted the text by denying altogether that any real resurrection took place. Others, wanting to guard against a conflict with 1 Corinthians 15:20, postpone this miracle until after Christ's resurrection, or say that the saints were not raised with immortal bodies. The first interpretation clearly contradicts the text which states that these saints 'were raised to life' and that 'they came out of the tombs ... and appeared to many people'. The other interpretations ignore the fact that the legal basis of these resurrections was still the death and resurrection of Christ. What matters is not the timing of their resurrection, but the certainty of Christ's. They also fail to do justice to the symbolic significance of this event, which prefigures the bodily resurrection of believers at Christ's second coming.

In our view the meaning of the text is that true believers, who had died before Christ's crucifixion, were raised from the dead with real, physical bodies at the time of Christ's death. After Jesus had been resurrected they went into Jerusalem and appeared to many people. Then they were taken up by God into heaven. Calvin admits the possibility that after confirming the hope of the heavenly life among those who were then alive, they again rested in their graves. But he goes on to say that 'it is more probable that the life which they received was not afterwards taken from them; for if it had been a mortal life, it would not have been proof of a perfect resurrection.' The end of Christ's life was the trumpet call for others to leave their graves and live for ever. Even in death Christ was the 'resurrection and the life' (John 11:25).

The resurrected saints are a symbol of the coming resurrection of all believers. They are a sign that every saint will be like them when the Lord Jesus returns from heaven with his holy ones. Death for the Christian is but a sleep of the body until that resurrection morning. It is a putting off of the trials and temptations that buffet our weak and corruptible bodies, and a passing over to the 'city with foundations, whose architect and builder is God' (Hebrews 11:10). Resurrection, on the other hand, is a putting on of our new glorious bodies that bear the likeness of Christ. Together they are an unclothing of all that we despise — impurity, disease, mortality — and an enrobing with the garments of holiness, power and glory. Then we shall declare to the glory of God: 'Death has been swallowed up in victory' (1 Corinthians 15:54).

If this is our hope of glory, what kind of people ought we to be? We ought to be kind and compassionate, forgiving and gentle, as we live to the praise of his glory. We ought to purify ourselves, just as our Saviour is pure, and to remind ourselves that if we are looking forward to being changed into his image in the twinkling of an eye, we must first prove by our upright and blameless lives that we have been made new by his power. If we believe that our lowly bodies will one day resemble Christ's glorious body, then we must daily offer ourselves to God as living sacrifices, and demonstrate by our obedience that we are already being 'transformed into his likeness with ever-increasing glory' (2 Corinthians 3:18). If we claim to live in Christ, we must walk as he did. Only then shall be made like him in death.

When the centurion and those with him who were guarding Jesus saw the earthquake and all that had happened, they were terrified, and exclaimed, 'Surely he was the Son of God!' (Matthew 27:54).

And when the centurion, who stood there in front of Jesus, heard his cry and saw how he died, he said, 'Surely this man was the Son of God!' (Mark 15:39).

The centurion, seeing what had happened, praised God and said, 'Surely this was a righteous man.' When all the people who had gathered to witness this sight saw what took place, they beat their breasts and went away. (Luke 23:47-48).

19.
The Centurion's Confession

It is a damning testimony against the Jewish religious leaders that a Roman soldier, who had enjoyed none of the advantages of God's people, should confess in such noble tones the divinity and innocence of Christ. He was a pagan, calloused by a life of godlessness and cruelty, yet he was moved to honour our Lord in a way that shamed their self-righteousness. Think of it — a Gentile, darkened in his understanding, ignorant of the Holy Scriptures, and separated from the life of God, acknowledged the Messiah, while the religious leaders, whose privileges included the adoption as sons, the divine glory, the covenants and the law, the temple worship and the promises and the patriarchs, and from whom is traced the human ancestry of Christ (Romans 9:4-5), spurned him outrageously.

Matthew writes that 'when the centurion and those with him who were guarding Jesus saw the earthquake and all that had happened, they were terrified and exclaimed, "Surely he was the Son of God" ' (27:54). Mark is a little more specific: 'When the centurion, who stood there in front of Jesus, heard his cry and saw how he died, he said, "Surely this man was the Son of God" ' (15:39). Luke mentions that the centurion 'praised God and said, "Surely this was a righteous man" ' (23:47).

Whether or not the centurion's confession was an act of saving faith is uncertain. There is little doubt that he was visibly affected by the earthquake and the other supernatural events of that day, but was he driven to Christ out of a desperate need for forgiveness? Was he simply amazed at the dignity displayed by a dying man, praising God for such an example of patient endurance in the midst of unmentionable sufferings, or was he confessing Christ as Lord and Saviour? Did he exhibit an outburst of only human emotion, giving intellectual assent to Christ's deity, or had the Holy Spirit opened his heart to see with the eyes of saving faith God's one and only Son?

Legend says he became a Christian. This is supported by the soldiers' use of the term 'Son of God'. This title was usually reserved for the Roman Emperor, who was worshipped in the state cult and who would not have wanted it to be applied to anyone else. It must have taken some courage therefore for a Roman centurion to use it to describe Jesus. If the centurion was professing Christ as his Lord and Saviour, it is a wonderful testimony to the power of the cross that it rescued a sinner so quickly.

Most commentators think the change was more transitory than permanent, more an outward display of wonder than an inward transformation of the heart. Calvin remarks that 'the centurion had not undergone such a change as to dedicate himself to God for the remainder of his life, but was only for a moment the herald of the divinity of Christ.' There is a world of difference from making a sudden and emotional statement of truth about Christ, to the deep and lasting work of the Holy Spirit that regenerates the soul. It is one thing to acknowledge Christ publicly after witnessing the terrors and mysteries of Calvary. It is quite another to fall at the foot of the cross in humiliation and repentance. It costs little to say, 'Surely he was the Son of God' (Matthew 27:54); it costs a life of devotion to serve Christ daily in a hostile world.

In today's church it is frequently the case that a raised arm in response to a preacher's pleas is deemed sufficient to save a soul from hell. Sometimes a few paces to the front of a building is evidence, so we are told, that a man has passed from death to life. There seems little of the old-fashioned conviction of sin, where men and women are bowed low under the agonising sense of their own guilt. When Jonathan Edwards was preaching his sermon *Sinners in the Hands of an Angry God* such was the presence of God that the congregation moaned and groaned under the burden of personal guilt. Many cried out such things as 'What shall I do to be saved?' An eye-witness reports that 'there was such a breathing of distress and weeping that the preacher was obliged to speak to the people and desire silence that he might be heard' (Aldridge). In many twentieth century churches those who want to become Christians are gently led through a *sinner's prayer*, often with little perception of God's awesome holiness or their own unworthiness.

Let us implore God for an outpouring of the Holy Spirit as on the day of Pentecost, when three thousand were cut to the heart and cried out for divine mercy! The Holy Spirit was not sent from heaven simply to comfort God's children in times of distress, but to 'convict the world of guilt in regard to sin and righteousness and judgement' (John 16:8). He sharpens the sword of the Spirit, which is the word of God, so it penetrates 'even to dividing soul and spirit, joints and marrow, and judges the thoughts and attitudes of the heart' (Hebrews 4:12). He exposes the filth of man's nature and convinces the wicked of their utter hopelessness without the saving grace of God. With force he opens our eyes to the hell we deserve, before drawing us with cords of love to Christ our Redeemer.

It seems that nature's reaction convinced the centurion and his men that the man who had just given up his spirit was who he claimed to be, the Son of God. They may not have realised the significance of his death or fully understood their own exclamation, but having heard the accusations of the chief priests, along with the scoffings of others, and witnessed Christ's response to it all, they were persuaded that Christ's testimony about himself was true. The centurion, who stood watching Jesus, was particularly moved by Christ's last words,

'Father, into your hands I commit my spirit' (Luke 23:46), and by the way he died. He had seen many men die, but it was the strength and faith and serenity of Christ at death that compelled him to glorify God. His cry may have been born from a mixture of pagan superstition and confused faith, rather than the saving work of God, as some suggest, nevertheless, it was sincere.

It is possible to make great statements of faith about Christ and to taste the goodness of the word of God and the powers of the coming age, and even to share in the Holy Spirit, yet remain outside the kingdom of heaven (Hebrews 6:4-5). In the parable of the sower Jesus mentions two groups of people who at first give the appearance of being saved. The first group receive the word with joy but fall away in the time of testing. The second group hear the word 'but as they go on their way they are choked by life's worries, riches and pleasures, and they do not mature' (Luke 8:14). It is not our initial response to the gospel or to the claims of Christ that heralds our salvation, but whether by persevering we produce a crop of obedience to the commands of God. Many jump with joy when they hear the message of the cross and all that it means, but they do not put into practice the words of Jesus: 'If anyone would come after me, he must deny himself and take up his cross daily and follow me' (Luke 9:23).

Simon the sorcerer was astonished by the great signs and miracles he saw Philip perform. He believed him as he preached the kingdom of God and the name of Jesus Christ, and was even baptised. He also saw Peter and John placing their hands on people, who immediately received the Holy Spirit. But when he tried to 'buy the gift of God with money', Peter saw through his duplicity and said, 'Your heart is not right before God ... For I see you are full of bitterness and captive to sin' (Acts 8:20-21,23). There was no one in a more privileged position than Judas Iscariot, who for three years walked with Jesus. Yet his treachery proved him to be 'the one doomed to destruction' (John 17:12). What counts is not an external show of Christianity, but 'faith expressing itself through love' (Galatians 5:6). And love for God is not just a feeling of affection for Christ. It is an ongoing commitment to follow God's word: 'This is love for God: to obey his commands' (1 John 5:3).

The Roman soldiers, who acknowledged Christ as the Son of God, are commonly recognised as a type of the calling of the Gentiles. Their confession at the cross is one of the first signs that Christ died for both Jews and Gentiles, and a fulfilment of God's promise to those who, up to this point, had been excluded from citizenship in Israel: 'I will call them "my people" who were not my people; and I will call her "my loved one" who is not my loved one;' and again, 'It will happen that in the very place where it was said to them, "You are not my people," they will be called "sons of the living God" ' (Romans 9:25-26).

What is surprising is not that Gentile soldiers praised the God of heaven and earth, but that the Jewish leaders continued to revile his Son. They should have been the first to recognise the Messiah and to rally to his side. They should have immediately exalted the Lord of glory, who had been sent to save the lost sheep of Israel. As it was pagan soldiers, who knew nothing of the predictions of the prophets, humiliated the chief priests by extolling the king of the Jews. How apt to our present case is the saying of Jesus: 'For judgement I have come into this world, so that the blind will see and those who see will become blind' (John 9:39).

Even the watching crowd was in some measure moved by the final hours of Christ's life. Luke records that 'when all the people who had gathered to witness this sight saw what took place, they beat their breasts and went away' (23:48). They wandered from the scene striking themselves in self-reproach for their part in crucifying an innocent man. Some went to Calvary out of curiosity. They left remorseful and heavy hearted. Others climbed that blessed hill to taunt a religious fanatic. They slunk away dumbfounded by all they had witnessed. Calvin remarks that their actions expressed 'the dread of punishment. They feared that something unhappy would befall their country as retribution for their having all consented to the unjust and shocking murder of Christ.'

Calvin goes on to say that 'since nothing more is described to us than the lamentation which God drew from them to the glory of his Son, let us learn by this example, that it is of little importance, or of no importance at all, if a man is struck with terror, when he sees before his eyes the power of God, until, after the astonishment has been abated, the fear of God remains calmly in his heart.' To beat one's breast from a sense of shame while turning away from Christ is a worldly sorrow that leads to death. The true penitent, no matter what he has done or how deep the guilt he feels, beats his breast as he kneels at the foot of the cross, pleading for forgiveness. 'Godly sorrow brings repentance that leads to salvation and leaves no regret' (2 Corinthians 7:10). One man thinks that self-abasement is sufficient to wash a stained conscience. Another knows that only the blood of Christ can cleanse him from all unrighteousness.

So the sad crowd wound its way slowly back to the city of Jerusalem to prepare for the Sabbath, leaving the centurion and his men, and a few women who stood watching from a distance, alone with Christ. There was nothing left for them to see. All was calm, and Christ was dead.

Now it was the day of Preparation, and the next day was to be a special Sabbath. Because the Jews did not want the bodies left on the crosses during the Sabbath, they asked Pilate to have the legs broken and the bodies taken down. The soldiers therefore came and broke the legs of the first man who had been crucified with Jesus, and then those of the other. But when they came to Jesus and found that he was already dead, they did not break his legs. Instead, one of the soldiers pierced Jesus' side with a spear, bringing a sudden flow of blood and water. The man who saw it has given testimony, and his testimony is true. He knows that he tells the truth, and he testifies so that you also may believe. These things happened so that the Scripture would be fulfilled, 'Not one of his bones will be broken,' and, as another Scripture says, 'They will look on the one they have pierced.' (John 19:31-37).

20.
The Final Indignity

'Now it was the day of Preparation, and the next day was to be a special Sabbath. Because the Jews did not want the bodies left on the crosses during the Sabbath, they asked Pilate to have the legs broken and the bodies taken down' (John 19:31). The day of Preparation was the day before the Sabbath. It was a Friday on which special preparations were made for one of the great days of the Jewish religious calendar, the Passover Sabbath, which began at 6:00pm that evening. The Passover itself lasted for seven days. The chief priests realised that if three bodies were left hanging on crosses during the Passover, overlooking the holy city of Jerusalem and in full view of the temple and its worshippers, the festival would be desecrated. They knew that Old Testament law demanded that a dead body must not remain on a tree overnight, but be taken down and buried the same day, 'because anyone who is hung on a tree is under God's curse' (Deuteronomy 21:23). They also knew that it was forbidden for them to touch or bury a dead body on the Sabbath. So they went to Pilate with their macabre request.

What shocking hypocrisy! These men prepared for one of the most holy days of the year, a day in which God was praised for his goodness, justice and power, with hands stained with the blood of the Son of God! They were more concerned about obeying various ceremonies than about the deliberate and callous murder of an innocent man. They were worried and upset in case they defiled themselves with a dead body, yet utterly careless of the guilt they had incurred for condemning their own Messiah.

Is there a more shameful example of the double standards of religious men, of hypocrites who make a show of obeying God only to ignore the demands of the moral law? Is there any other request that is so despicable in its flagrant disregard of justice? It is an illustration of an outward religion that excludes God. It is men pretending to obey the letter of the law while rejecting the Spirit of holiness and truth. It is ceremony before justice and law without mercy. J.C. Ryle, first bishop of Liverpool, rightly remarks that 'we see men making ado about a dead body remaining on the cross on the Sabbath, at the very time when they had just murdered an innocent living person with the most flagrant injustice and monstrous cruelty. It is a specimen of "straining out a gnat and swallowing a camel"' (Matthew 23:24).

The chief priests went to Pilate, the Roman governor, and asked him to have the legs of the three men broken and the bodies taken down from the crosses. The breaking of the legs was a customary form of accelerating death known as *crurifragium*. It was a punishment that was almost as harsh and brutal as the crucifixion itself. (Some historians say that it was not the breaking of the legs that accelerated death, but the shock that attended such cruelty.) The soldiers responsible used a heavy hammer, perhaps the one with which they had driven in the nails, or an iron club, to shatter the bones in the legs. With this request the chief priests were hoping to remove Christ 'out of sight and mind' of the people. They wanted to extinguish the threat he posed to their authority, and to celebrate the Sabbath with a 'clear conscience'.

Through this hypocrisy, which is worthy of the severest condemnation, we see the providential hand of God working for the praise of his glory. If the Jews had not gone to Pilate, the Romans would not only have left the bodies on the crosses for several days until putrefied or consumed by birds of prey, but would also have forbidden their proper burial. Thus David's prophecy: 'Nor will you let your Holy One see decay' (Psalm 16:10; cf Acts 2:27) would not have been fulfilled. Similarly, because the Jews procured the burial of our Lord on the same day as his death, it meant that in accordance with his own word he was buried (Matthew 26:12) and remained 'three days and three nights in the heart of the earth' (Matthew 12:40). Thereafter, on the third day, he was raised to life as he had predicted (Matthew 20:19). This would not have happened if the Jews had not interfered.

The penitent thief, to whom Christ had promised: 'Today you will be with me in paradise' (Luke 23:43), had to endure one last act of brutality before he passed through the pearly gates. The saving grace of God did not prevent this final agony. Just because we are members of the body of Christ does not mean we are exempt from bodily sufferings or from the trials and hardships that are common to the world. There are poor, downcast and afflicted Christians just as there are poor, downcast and afflicted infidels. Our redemption does not entitle us to a life free from the heartaches and physical ailments that oppress others. What it does entitle us to is an access into the presence of God where grace and mercy are found to support us in our time of need. It assures us that in all things — in trouble, persecution, famine, nakedness, danger or sword — we are more than conquerors and that in all creation there is nothing to separate us from the love of God that is in Christ Jesus our Lord (Romans 8:35-39). When the soldiers stood ready to break the penitent's legs, he knew that paradise was only a moment away.

'The soldiers therefore came and broke the legs of the first man who had been crucified with Jesus, and then those of the other. But when they came to Jesus and found that he was already dead, they did not break his legs' (John 19:32). It is often asked why the soldiers broke the legs of the two thieves before going to Christ. There are several possible reasons: The two outer crosses were stationed further forward than the centre cross so the three crucified men could look at each other; it was therefore only natural to go to the nearer crosses first. Two pairs of soldiers went to the outer crosses simultaneously, leaving the cross of Christ until last. The soldiers, who had witnessed Christ's final word from the cross and watched as he 'bowed his head' (John 19:30), suspected he was already dead; so they dealt with the thieves before turning their attention more directly to him. The centurion, who had earlier professed faith in Christ, dissuaded the soldiers from breaking his legs. Perhaps the hand of God restrained them from further afflicting the body of his Son.

When the soldiers came to Jesus and examined him, they found that he was already dead. So the effort of breaking the legs was rendered unnecessary. These soldiers, who were professional and experienced executioners, would not have disobeyed Pilate's orders unless they were sure Christ had expired.

Instead of breaking Christ's legs, 'one of the soldiers pierced Jesus' side with a spear, bringing a sudden flow of blood and water' (John 19:34). This last and crowning indignity of thrusting a lance into our Lord's heart was not the cause of his death, for he had already given up his spirit (John 19:30), but it was an act that made death absolutely certain. Someone has remarked that the spear was guided by the Father's hand so as to leave us in no doubt that Christ died as a sacrifice of atonement.

A great deal has been written about the blood and water that flowed from Christ's side. One plausible theory is that Christ's death 'resulted from rupture of the heart in consequence of great mental agony and sorrow. Such a death would be almost instantaneous. The blood flowing into the pericardium would coagulate into the red clot (blood) and the limpid serum (water). This blood and water would then be released by the spear thrust' (Hendriksen). There is no question that Christ suffered intense and unequalled agony of mind on behalf of sinners which could have caused this physiological state. However, many theologians and physicians do not accept this explanation. Some, who find all the various theories untenable, simply say it was a special and inexplicable miracle.

There are also numerous spiritual interpretations of the water and blood. These range from a symbolization of the two sacraments, the Lord's Supper and baptism, to a symbolic fulfilment of Zechariah's prophecy: 'On that day a fountain will be opened to the house of David and the inhabitants of Jerusalem, to cleanse them from sin and impurity' (13:1). In the Old Testament blood is the symbol of atonement and water is the symbol of cleansing, so any interpretation must include these two. Matthew Henry comments: 'The blood and water signified the two great benefits which all believers partake of through Christ — justification and sanctification. Blood stands for remission, water for regeneration; blood for atonement, water for purification. The two must always go together as both flowed from the pierced side of our Redeemer.' It is as if a river of life flowed to all the elect from the side of our Lord — the blood to take away our sins and pacify an angry and offended God, the water to make us new and acceptable to a holy Saviour.

This episode made a very deep impression on the apostle John, who had probably returned to the cross after conducting Mary to his own home in obedience to Christ's word (John 19:27). He makes a solemn declaration that as an eye-witness 'his testimony is true' and worthy of full acceptance. He then states the reason for testifying: 'that you also may believe' (John 19:35) in the Son of God who died to 'save his people from their sins' (Matthew 1:21). He wants us to embrace the God-Man as our personal Saviour and to follow him wherever he leads. In the following chapter he confirms this desire when, talking about the miracles of Christ, he says, 'These are written that you may believe that Jesus is the Christ, the Son of God, and that by believing you may have life in his name' (20:31).

What greater blessing can we bestow on lost souls than to point them to Christ, 'who gave himself for us to redeem us from all wickedness and to purify for himself a people that are his very own' (Titus 2:14)? It is to our shame that often we appear content to leave our friends and family aimlessly wandering in a spiritual wilderness. Is it because we are afraid of offending them that we fail to usher them to Calvary? Perhaps we imagine that because our neighbour is so ungodly in his attitudes and actions that he lies outside the reach of the cross. We forget that Christ died for sinners and that our lives were just as depraved not so long ago. Let us pray that God would once again send out workers into the harvest field to reap souls for his kingdom. Many members in today's church often sit idly by, playing with a host of excuses as to why they cannot proclaim Christ to the lost. 'Nobody in the modern world is interested,' they claim. 'It is the age of irreligion. We're too busy serving Christ in other areas. Let the paid ministers get on with it—it's their job! I'm too reserved to share my faith...' and so on. If only men and women would be so taken up with Christ that nothing in all the world could stop them from speaking of his grace! Let us ask God to raise up more men in the mould of Paul, who was compelled by Christ's love to preach the gospel.

When we know Christ, deeply and intimately, our hearts will long to share him with others and to bring them under the shadow of his wing. A weak faith is the precursor to a weak witness. A lack of the knowledge of God curtails the power of a believer's testimony. Our constant prayer should be for an outpouring of the Spirit of wisdom and revelation so that we may know God better, not just in an academic sense, but in a way that changes our lives and equips us to serve him without compromise or fear.

John confirms our faith in his testimony by citing the Old Testament: 'These things happened so that the Scripture would be fulfilled, "Not one of his bones will be broken," and, as another Scripture says, "They will look on the one they have pierced"' (John 19:36-37). The first Scripture is taken from Exodus 12:46 (cf Numbers 9:12; Psalm 34:20), where God imposes certain restrictions on the Israelites regarding the Passover. One of these restrictions forbade the Israelites to break the bones of the Passover lamb, which was a type of Christ (1 Corinthians 5:7). It is true to say that even if all the hosts of heaven and earth had descended on Christ with the express intention of breaking his legs, not one of them would have been able to crack a single bone. The aims of the Jews, the order of Pilate, the willingness of the soldiers to obey their governor, were all in vain, for God had determined otherwise. It was God's will to save his Son from this final atrocity and it was God's will that prevailed.

It is futile for the wicked to try and oppose or reverse God's will, or for them to imagine that their intentions can nullify his purpose. 'In his heart a man plans his course, but the Lord determines his steps' (Proverbs 16:9). 'Many are the plans in a man's heart, but it is the Lord's purpose that prevails' (Proverbs 19:21). 'There is no wisdom, no insight, no plan that can succeed against the Lord' (Proverbs 21:30). These three Scriptures alone should be enough to convince us that God works out everything in conformity with the purpose of his will. No matter how hard the godless try or how many fight for their cause, only God's plans will prosper. Such an understanding of God's sovereign power is like a safety net against the mistakes, failings and sins that fill our lives. It is our hope that righteousness will ultimately triumph.

The second Scripture John quotes is from Zechariah 12:10, where the Lord declares, 'I will pour out on the house of David and the inhabitants of Jerusalem a spirit of grace and supplication. They will look on me, the one they have pierced, and mourn for him as one mourns for an only child, and grieve bitterly for him as one grieves for a firstborn son.' This prophecy was fulfilled, at least partially, when the Roman soldier thrust a spear into our Lord's side in full view of the watching Jews. Many of these Jews subsequently went away beating their breasts in self-contempt for their part in the murder of Christ.

There is, though, a much broader fulfilment of the prophecy. In one sense the prophecy is fulfilled every time a sinner, Jew or Gentile, calls on the name of the Lord; for to 'look on the one they have pierced' means to look with remorse for their share in his death, and for their guilt before God. It was fulfilled on the day of Pentecost when three thousand turned to the Lord in repentance and faith. It is fulfilled throughout the world whenever a man, woman or child looks with a broken and contrite spirit on the crucified Messiah. It will be fulfilled when 'all Israel' is saved (Romans 11:26), and again at the end of the Christian era when every Jew and Gentile, including those who remain in obstinate unbelief, 'will see him, even those who pierced him; and all the peoples of the earth will mourn because of him' (Revelation 1:7).

Yes, our Lord was pierced. He was pierced by the crown of thorns thrust upon his brow. He was pierced by the nails so crudely driven into his hands and feet. He was pierced by the spear forced into his side, and pierced by us and for us whose sin condemned him to the cross. With humble adoration let us sing in a loud voice with the angels of heaven: 'Worthy is the Lamb, who was slain, to receive power and wealth and wisdom and strength and honour and glory and praise!' (Revelation 5:12). Let us bow before him who has redeemed us from an empty and meaningless way of life. Let us live in him and look to him, overflowing with thankfulness and offering him a service that never tires, and a worship that is always sincere.

So Christ's limp and lifeless body hung on the cross, waiting for the timely intervention of Joseph of Arimathea. How long exactly it remained there, we do not know, nor is it important. Already the whole of creation was looking forward, beyond the cross, to the first day of the week when all heaven would rejoice at the sound of the angel's words to the women: 'Do not be afraid, for I know you are looking for Jesus, who was crucified. He is not here; he has risen, just as he said' (Matthew 28:5-6). But first he had to be taken down from the cross and buried...

The Burial

As evening approached, there came a rich man from Arimathea, named Joseph, who had himself become a disciple of Jesus. Going to Pilate, he asked for Jesus' body, and Pilate ordered that it be given to him. Joseph took the body, wrapped it in a clean linen cloth, and placed it in his own new tomb that he had cut out of the rock. He rolled a big stone in front of the entrance to the tomb and went away. (Matthew 27:57-60).

It was Preparation Day (that is, the day before the Sabbath). So as evening approached, a prominent member of the Council, who was himself waiting for the kingdom of God, went boldly to Pilate and asked for Jesus' body. Pilate was surprised to hear that he was already dead. Summoning the centurion, he asked him if Jesus had already died. When he learned from the centurion that it was so, he gave the body to Joseph. So Joseph brought some linen cloth, took down the body, wrapped it in the linen, and placed it in a tomb cut out of rock. Then he rolled a stone against the entrance of the tomb. (Mark 15:42-46).

Now there was a man named Joseph, a member of the Council, a good and upright man, who had not consented to their decision and action. He came from the Judean town of Arimathea and he was waiting for the kingdom of God. Going to Pilate, he asked for Jesus' body. Then he took it down, wrapped it in linen cloth and placed it in a tomb cut in the rock, one in which no one had yet been laid. It was Preparation Day, and the Sabbath was about to begin. (Luke 23:50-54).

Later, Joseph of Arimathea asked Pilate for the body of Jesus. Now Joseph was a disciple of Jesus, but secretly because he feared the Jews. With Pilate's permission, he came and took the body. He was accompanied by Nicodemus, the man who earlier had visited Jesus at night. Nicodemus brought a mixture of myrrh and aloes, about seventy-five pounds. Taking Jesus' body, the two of them wrapped it, with the spices, in strips of linen. This was in accordance with Jewish burial customs. At the place where Jesus was crucified, there was a garden, and in the garden a new tomb, in which no one had ever been laid. Because it was the Jewish day of Preparation and since the tomb was near by, they laid Jesus there. (John 19:38-42).

21.
Joseph of Arimathea and Nicodemus

The crowd had drifted slowly away, some beating their breasts, others keeping their thoughts and grief to themselves. A few people though most of whom were remained by the cross: a number of faithful women who had followed Jesus from Galilee to care for his needs; the soldiers, most of whom were indifferent to all that had taken place; the centurion, whose confession of faith had pierced the dark sky; others who knew Christ were silently waiting; and the thieves, whose mangled legs hung limply and whose final groans disturbed the peace, sank into the sleep of death. The friends who remained watched quietly, hardly able to believe what had taken place.

Again we are told it was the 'Jewish day of Preparation' (John 19:42), that is, the day before the Sabbath. Luke writes that the 'Sabbath was about to begin' (23:54). Both Matthew and Mark note that evening was approaching (27:57; 15:42). We do not know the exact time, but it must have been fairly close to 6:00pm, the hour the Sabbath began. Whatever had to be done with the body of Jesus, had to be done quickly, so that the Sabbath would not be violated or the land desecrated according to Old Testament law (Deuteronomy 21:23).

It is only after the death of Jesus that we are introduced to Joseph of Arimathea, whose office of kindness to our Lord is for ever remembered. We may forget the love others show us.

Even some of the blessings God lavishes on us may slip our minds. But the Lord never forgets the service we render to him or the succour and support we give to his children. 'God is not unjust; he will not forget your work and the love you have shown him as you have helped his people and continue to help them' (Hebrews 6:10). Joseph was from Arimathea, a Judean town, probably Ramathaim-Zophim on Mount Ephraim, which was the birth place of the prophet Samuel (1 Samuel 1:1). It was approximately twenty-four miles northwest of Jerusalem. Joseph was a 'prominent member of the Council' (Mark 15:43); that is, he was an important and influential member of the Sanhedrin, the Jewish supreme court. He was a man of standing, whose views were well respected and whose counsel was often sought. Luke calls him a 'good and upright man, who had not consented to their decision and action' (23:50-51). He had not agreed with the other members of the Sanhedrin in their condemnation of Christ, probably absenting himself from the meeting, so as to avoid having to voice his dissent publicly. John says he 'was a disciple of Jesus, but secretly because he feared the Jews' (19:38). He was afraid that if he followed Christ openly, he would be thrown out of the Sanhedrin and the synagogue, for 'the Jews had decided that anyone who acknowledged that Jesus was the Christ would be put out of the synagogue' (John 9:22; cf.12:42). At this stage Joseph loved praise from men more than praise from God.

There is always a price to pay in following Jesus. It may simply be that our old friends forsake us, or our families whisper their disapproval behind our backs. Perhaps our workmates laugh at us occasionally and make the odd snide remark. More seriously, though, it could mean physical persecution such as imprisonment and torture, or even a slow and cruel death. Sadly there are many believers in the world today who are suffering terribly at the hands of wicked men.

Any sort of persecution is deplorable and must be rigorously and publicly condemned, but it should not catch us unawares.

Paul says that 'everyone who wants to live a godly life will be persecuted' (2 Timothy 3:12). The question to ask ourselves is not 'Why am I being unjustly treated?' but 'Am I being persecuted for Christ's sake?' If we suffer, it should not be 'as a murderer or thief or any other kind of criminal, or even as a meddler' (1 Peter 4:15), but as a Christian. If, however, we are not suffering for the cause of the gospel, but living a life of ease, without enemies or troubles, we must ask ourselves: 'Are we following Christ with the wholehearted devotion that he demands and deserves?'

The fear of man is a snare that traps the faint hearted. If we are not careful, we might be deceived into thinking that a silent testimony is all that is necessary. A silent testimony though is often no testimony at all. If we are living an upright, moral life without any reference to Christ, how are we different from so many men and women whose principles are commendable but who have no faith in Christ? All we are doing is testifying to ourselves and reaping the world's applause. Jesus said, 'Woe to you when all men speak well of you, for that is how their fathers treated the false prophets' (Luke 6:26). An invisible faith or a faith that never expresses itself is a sham, and a denial of God's word. To hide our light under a bowl is to hide Christ under a bowl. To deny in public what we profess in the privacy of our hearts is to try and have one foot on the rock of our salvation and the other on the sinking sands of Satan's kingdom. Vacillation in the Christian walk makes us unstable in all we do and an unworthy representative of Christ.

Joseph was a 'rich man' (Matthew 27:57), who unwittingly fulfilled Isaiah's prophecy that the Christ would be 'assigned a grave with the wicked, and with the rich in his death' (53:9). Riches in themselves cannot prevent a man coming to faith in Christ, but they do obstruct the path to salvation with manifold temptations. They parade the world's pleasures before our eyes, and in so doing encourage us to live a life of self-sufficiency. After speaking with a rich young ruler who refused to forsake his wealth for the treasures of heaven, Jesus said, 'It is easier for a camel to go through the eye of a needle than for a rich man to enter the kingdom of God' (Matthew 19:24). It is of course impossible for a camel, however small, to squeeze through the tiny eye of a needle. Recognizing this, the disciples exclaimed, 'Who then can be saved?' (Matthew 19:25). Jesus replied, 'With man this is impossible, but with God all things are possible' (Matthew 19:26).

Joseph was also 'waiting for the kingdom of God' (Mark 15:43). He was looking expectantly for the Messiah's advent coupled with the spiritual reign of God in people's hearts. In many respects he was like Simeon who was 'waiting for the consolation of Israel' (Luke 2:25), or Anna who 'spoke about the child to all who were looking forward to the redemption of Jerusalem' (Luke 2:38). However, before we highlight Joseph's part in the gospel story, we ought, as Calvin says, 'first to consider the providence of God, in subduing a man of high and honourable rank among his countrymen, to wipe away the reproach of the cross by the honour of burial.'

As evening approached Joseph 'went boldly to Pilate and asked for Jesus' body' (Mark 15:43). He knew that time was short, for the Sabbath was about to begin, so casting his fear aside he strode courageously and openly into Pilate's presence, hoping to secure the body of his Saviour for burial. In doing so, he exposed himself not only to the scorn of a Jew-hating Roman governor, but also to the animosity of the Sanhedrin who were bound to hear of his actions. He was prepared, despite the obvious dangers, to lose his reputation and status for the sake of his Master. But what had brought about the change in Joseph? What had turned a man of feeble faith, who had followed Jesus secretly for fear of the Jews, into someone who unashamedly publicized his devotion to the One who had died for him? What had made the difference? In a word, the cross — the cross had emboldened him to serve anew his Lord. The miracles of Calvary, the inscription above Christ's head, the seven words of the cross uttered by our Lord, the dignity of Christ in suffering and in death — all this had challenged and strengthened his faith, and had proved it to be genuine.

Fear is no inhibitor to God. Peter in his own strength fled from Christ and denied him three times, but when empowered by God he stood up before thousands to proclaim the death and resurrection of Christ. Paul approached the Corinthians in 'weakness and fear, and with much trembling', but God demonstrated the Spirit's power through his preaching (1 Corinthians 2:3-4). When the feeblest believer is touched by God's Spirit, nothing is impossible for him. On the first Easter Day the 'disciples were together, with the doors locked for fear of the Jews' (John 20:19). But after the day of Pentecost, when they were 'filled with the Holy Spirit' (Acts 2:4), they courageously proclaimed Christ to the world and laid down their lives in his service.

At first Pilate was surprised to hear that Jesus had already died, for death by crucifixion was usually a very slow process. (The breaking of the legs was designed to accelerate and guarantee death, not to cause it.) So he summoned the centurion and 'asked him if Jesus had already died. When he learned from the centurion that it was so, he gave the body to Joseph' (Mark 15:44-45). Van Doren, an American clergyman, makes the point that 'the centurion who executed the decree of Pilate, the friends who took him from the cross, the women who beheld the lifeless corpse, the priests who sealed the grave and set a watch, the soldiers who guarded the sepulchre are all witnesses to his death.'

With the governor's permission, Joseph with some linen cloth in hand 'came and took the body' (John 19:38). The cross was laid flat on the ground. The nails were twisted out of the hands and feet by the soldiers, and the bloody and mangled corpse handed over to Joseph. John reports that 'he was accompanied by Nicodemus, the man who had earlier visited Jesus at night' (19:39). Nicodemus was also a rich 'member of the Jewish ruling council' (John 3:1). Like Joseph he had been afraid to declare publicly his faith in Christ. It is not clear whether he had gone with Joseph to Pilate but he was certainly at hand to help Joseph with the body of Jesus. He 'brought a mixture of myrrh and aloes, about seventy-five pounds' (John 19:39), in order to embalm the body. At this point neither Nicodemus nor Joseph expected Christ to rise from the dead, nor did they consider him incorruptible, although both knew the words of David in Psalm 16:10: 'You will not abandon me to the grave, nor will you let your Holy One see decay' (cf Acts 2:27).

'Taking Jesus' body, the two of them wrapped it, with the spices, in strips of linen. This was in accordance with Jewish burial customs' (John 19:40). With loving devotion and reverent care the two men washed the body of Jesus before tightly wrapping it limb by limb in the linen cloth with the mixture of myrrh and aloes strewn in. Then they carried it to Joseph's 'own new tomb that he had cut out of the rock' (Matthew 27:60). John describes the location of the tomb in a little more detail: 'At the place where Jesus was crucified, there was a garden, and in the garden a new tomb, in which no one had ever been laid. Because it was the Jewish day of Preparation and since the tomb was near by, they laid Jesus there' (19:41-42). Finally Joseph 'rolled a big stone in front of the entrance to the tomb and went away' (Matthew 27:60). The tomb was probably very close to the site assigned to it in the Church of the Holy Sepulchre.

Jesus was not thrown into a ditch or dumped in a common burial ground like many of the victims of crucifixion, but honourably laid in a new tomb, especially marked by God as the resting place for his Son's body. The tomb had been cut out of the side of limestone rock by one of his disciples. Inside part of the floor was hewn out a little lower for Christ's body to rest in. One of the surprising aspects of Christ's burial is that it was an act of piety performed by two men who were members of a religious group whose behaviour Jesus had severely condemned when alive. The hypocrisy of the Pharisees and their envy and hatred of Christ is well documented in the sacred record. It is therefore all the more remarkable that God should choose two of their number to care for his Son in death.

Van Doren sums up the burial of Christ when he says that the 'soldiers' insults are followed by tenderest attentions of refined friendship; the scourge, the buffet, the spittle, by spices and delicate perfumes; the mock robe and thorny crown, by pure white linen and a new tomb.'

Mary Magdalene and the other Mary were sitting there across from the tomb. (Matthew 27:61).

Mary Magdalene and Mary the mother of Joses saw where he was laid. (Mark 15:47).

The women who had come with Jesus from Galilee followed Joseph and saw the tomb and how his body was laid in it. Then they went home and prepared spices and perfumes. But they rested on the Sabbath in obedience to the commandment. (Luke 23:55-56).

22.
The Two Marys

The faithful women, who had not forsaken their Master in his hour of need, 'followed Joseph and saw the tomb and how his body was laid in it' (Luke 23:55). Among them were Mary Magdalene and Mary the mother of Joses and James. They were 'sitting there across from the tomb' (Matthew 27:61). They saw how Jesus' body was unnailed from the cross and how Joseph and Nicodemus carefully wrapped the corpse, with the spices, in clean linen cloth. They followed as the two men lovingly carried the body to the tomb, gently laying it to rest, before rolling the stone in front of the entrance, hiding for ever, or so they thought, the body of their Saviour. These women loved Christ in life, when the future was full of hope, and in death when all seemed lost. They wanted to be near Christ in the day of blessing and to stand by his side during the cursed night. They supported him when the world worshipped and when it abused and scorned. They yearned to express their devotion for him in whatever way they could, whatever the circumstances. That is why they had joined the victory ride into Jerusalem, and marched so readily up the hill of Calvary. That is why they made the journey of death to the tomb.

What were they thinking as they watched the Lord of life laid to rest in the grave? Could they picture in their minds the day when Jesus had raised the widow's son to life at Nain, and the amazement and joy on his mother's face as she received back her beloved? Could they hear him calling in a loud voice,

'Lazarus, come out!' and the gasps that greeted the dead man as he hobbled out of the grave, his hands and feet still wrapped with strips of linen, and a cloth around his face? Did they remember the words of hope that came from Jesus' lips, 'I am the resurrection and the life' (John 11:25)? Were they confused as they tried to reconcile them with his burial? Did they wonder why he had promised them so much, knowing that death by crucifixion would soon overtake him? Did they lift their heads to heaven and with deep sadness in their hearts whisper, 'Why, Lord?'

There are many temptations and perplexities that surround us when tragedy strikes. We are persuaded by advisors to search for reasons and to apportion blame. We struggle to understand why and ask ourselves, 'What good can possibly come from this?' We look for the purpose of God and end up bewildered and forlorn. We seek wise counsel and are given contradictory views that plunge us into deeper despair. We try to pray but have nothing to say. We read the Scriptures, but to our dismay no word comforts us. Guilt descends upon us like a cloud and weighs us down. There seems no way out as our days turn to night and the sound of laughter is heard no more.

The women by the tomb must have experienced all kinds of conflicting emotions and asked many unanswerable questions. Their souls were downcast and their Lord was dead. What could they do? Wait! Wait for the Lord. Wait just a few hours and Christ would rise from the dead. Wait and the gloom and despair that flooded their hearts would be swallowed up by an everlasting joy. Wait and Jesus, for whom they had shed many tears, would again walk by their side and speak to them the words of eternal life. Wait! It is sometimes so hard to do, but on the other side of the desert are green pastures and valleys filled with refreshing streams. We know that when the sun sinks at night, it rises again in the morning. When it hides behind a cloud, it soon reappears. Though our tears wet the pillow at night, a new day of laughter is about to dawn. After the storm, the sea is calm. Wait for the Lord. 'He gives strength to the weary and increases the power of the weak. Even youths grow tired and weary, and young men stumble and fall; but those who hope in the LORD will renew their strength. They will soar on wings like eagles; they will run and not grow weary, they will walk and not be faint' (Isaiah 40:29-31).

On Sunday morning the women's doubts and fears were answered and their hope restored a hundred fold. All those confusions that had befuddled their minds by the tomb, disappeared before the rising sun on that first Easter Day. The desperation that had squeezed their faith relinquished its hold, and a deeper, more certain confidence in God arose. The 'Why, Lord?' was drowned out by praises to the Saviour of the world. But before the trumpet of victory sounds, the funeral dirge must play. Before the ear of wheat produces many seeds, it must fall to the ground and die. Before the glory of the resurrection, the torture of the cross and the darkness of the grave.

Luke tells us that after the stone had been rolled against the entrance of the tomb, the women 'went home and prepared spices and perfumes. But they rested on the Sabbath in obedience to the commandment' (23:56). It may be that Joseph and Nicodemus had started to embalm the body of Jesus but, because the Sabbath was about to begin, had left the process unfinished. If that was the case the women were preparing to complete the embalming after the Sabbath. Or it may be that the women wanted to add spices and perfumes as their own act of devotion to Christ. Like Joseph and Nicodemus they had no hope of the resurrection at this stage.

The women must have been desperate to attend the body of Christ and to perfect the embalming; but they rested on the Sabbath so as not to disobey the Word of God. They were eager to serve Christ, but were not prepared to sin to do it. Many excuse disobedience by claiming it is for the good of others. 'The end justifies the means' is often cited to ease a stricken conscience. But is it right to rob the rich in order to feed the poor? Is it commendable in God's sight to fiddle our taxes so we can increase our tithe? Should we drink too much so that we can better share the gospel with drunkards? Is that what Paul meant when he said, 'I have become all things to all men so that by all possible means I might save some' (1 Corinthians 9:22)? Of course not! Our responsibility is to feed the poor without robbing the rich, to pay our taxes and our tithe, to share the gospel with all men without sharing in their sin.

Our obedience to God is far more important than the service we render him or the gifts we offer on his altar. After Saul had disobeyed the word of the Lord in order to present sacrifices to him, Samuel said, 'Does the LORD delight in burnt offerings and sacrifices as much as in obedience to the voice of the LORD? To obey is better than to sacrifice, and to heed is better than the fat of rams' (1 Samuel 15:22). God is not after our time or our money or our possessions. He demands our obedience. He wants our love for him to overflow in a willing and joyful adherence to his commands. He rejoices far more over one of his children who cheerfully obeys him, than over a host of men who make great sacrifices in his name but ignore his word. Without obedient love for God we are nothing but a resounding gong or a clanging cymbal, even if we do surrender our bodies to the flames for some noble cause. Love for God and obedience to his commands are the two legs that enable a Christian to stand.

The next day, the one after Preparation Day, the chief priests and the Pharisees went to Pilate. 'Sir,' they said, 'we remember that while he was still alive that deceiver said, "After three days I will rise again." So give the order for the tomb to be made secure until the third day. Otherwise, his disciples may come and steal the body and tell the people that he has been raised from the dead. This last deception will be worse than the first.'

'Take a guard,' Pilate answered. 'Go, make the tomb as secure as you know how.' So they went and made the tomb secure by putting a seal on the stone and posting a guard. (Matthew 27:62-66).

23.
The Sealing of the Tomb

On the Sabbath of the Passover the chief priests and Pharisees went to Pilate. 'Sir,' they said, 'we remember that while he was still alive that deceiver said, "After three days I will rise again." So give the order for the tomb to be made secure until the third day. Otherwise, his disciples may come and steal the body and tell the people that he has been raised from the dead. This last deception will be worse than the first' (Matthew 27:62-64). The chief priests and pharisees, who had so harshly condemned Jesus for healing the sick on the Sabbath, went to a heathen governor, who hated the Jews, on one of the most holy days of the religious year, the Passover Sabbath, and asked him to help them seal and guard the tomb of their own Messiah! It is an illustration of the Sanhedrin having one rule for themselves and another rule for everyone else! They allowed themselves to desecrate the Sabbath with impunity, but woe to their 'inferiors' who behaved likewise. They lived as they pleased, but forced all and sundry to obey without compromise their own harsh Pharisaical traditions. They should have followed the example of the women and 'rested on the Sabbath in obedience to the commandments' (Luke 23:56).

The chief priests and Pharisees courteously addressed Pilate as 'Sir', while referring derogatorily to Jesus as 'that deceiver'. How sad that they honoured a man who despised them and in the same breath slandered the Lord of love! Would Pilate have poured out his life for the lost sheep of Israel? Did he travel through all the towns and villages of Palestine, 'teaching in their synagogues, preaching the good news of the kingdom and healing every kind of disease and sickness'? (Matthew 9:35). Would he have humbled himself before his subjects and suffered at the hands of the people he had come to save? Could he have withstood the wrath of God against the sins of the world, or endured the torments of hell for sinners?

It was damnable blindness that persuaded the chief priests and Pharisees to speak of the Messiah in such blasphemous terms. What contempt from men who had witnessed the power of God in the works of Jesus and heard the words of heaven from his lips! They had seen the miracles of Calvary and watched the Saviour die on the cross. 'If our gospel is veiled,' says Paul, 'it is veiled to those who are perishing. The god of this age has blinded the minds of unbelievers, so that they cannot see the light of the gospel of the glory of Christ, who is the image of God' (2 Corinthians 4:3-4). If we have tasted the goodness of the Word of God and the powers of the coming age, yet remain in unbelief, what conclusion should we draw about our eternal destiny? Are we on a pilgrimage to heaven or treading the broad road that leads to hell?

Interestingly the chief priests asked for the tomb to be secured until 'the third day'. This coincided with the 'three days' of Jesus' prediction about his resurrection. They pleaded with Pilate to commission his soldiers to guard the tomb. Any attempt therefore by the disciples to fabricate Christ's resurrection by stealing his body could be easily resisted by armed and trained men. What they had failed to realise was that the last thing on the disciples' minds was the resurrection of Jesus. They were not expecting to see Jesus again. Even when the women reported that he had risen from the dead 'they did not believe ... because their words seemed to them like nonsense' (Luke 24:11). Jesus himself rebuked the Eleven 'for their lack of faith and their stubborn refusal to believe those who had seen him after he had risen' (Mark 16:14). It appears from

Matthew's account that the chief priests and Pharisees had a more complete understanding of the resurrection of Christ than the disciples!

Pilate, in his usual weak and purposeless fashion, granted the petition of Christ's enemies. " 'Take a guard," he said. "Go, make the tomb as secure as you know how." So they went and made the tomb secure by putting a seal on the stone and posting a guard' (Matthew 27:65-66). We do not know why Pilate submitted to the demands of the Sandhedrin. Perhaps he was so fed up with the whole affair that naything was permissible so long as it did not affect or impinge on his authority. Under the supervision of the priests, the guard was posted and 'a cord covered with clay or wax on which (Pilate's) official seal had been impressed was affixed to the stone at the grave's entrance' (Hendriksen).

It is ludicrous to think that these measures would hold Christ in the grave. They did however stop any supposed deception by the disciples. For even if the disciples had wanted to steal the body, they could not have overcome armed Roman soldiers, or moved the 'very large' stone (Mark 16:4) from the entrance of the tomb and then carried the corpse to a secret hideout without alerting the watching guard. And who among the frightened disciples would have had the courage to break the Roman governor's seal? The chief priests, by preventing any interference from the disciples, were authenticating the resurrection of Christ. Thanks to their efforts, the only explanation of the disappearance of Christ's body from the tomb is: 'He has risen, just as he said' (Matthew 28:6). J.C.Ryle says that 'their seal, their guard, their precautions, were all to become witnesses, in a few hours, that Christ had risen. They might as well have tried to stop the tides of the sea, or to prevent the sun rising, as to prevent Jesus coming forth from the tomb. They were taken in their own craftiness. Their own devices became instruments to show forth God's glory.'

'The One enthroned in heaven laughs; the Lord scoffs at them' (Psalm 2:4). He mocks the schemes of the wicked by using them to accomplish his own purpose. Those who oppose him neither understand his power nor see the futility of their feeble machinations. The sons of Jacob did all they could to prevent Joseph's dreams from coming true, yet when they sold their brother to the Ishmaelites for twenty shekels of silver, they began to fulfill those dreams themselves. The chief priests were God's servants, sent by him to prove to a sceptical world that the man they had crucified had indeed risen from the dead. They were moved by the hand of Almighty God to glorify his Son. The words of Joseph to his brothers when he was in charge of the whole land of Egypt also apply to them: 'You intended to harm me, but God intended it for good to accomplish what is now being done, the saving of many lives' (Genesis 50:20).

After the resurrection, the priests presented a large sum of money to the soldiers, telling them, 'You are to say, "His disciples came during the night and stole him away while we were asleep"' (Matthew 28:13). The chief priests, who had already charged Christ with deception, concocted a story with which to deceive Pilate, and in the same breath as they accused the disciples of stealing the body, they bribed others to circulate lies! The wickedness of the human heart is unfathomable! It is 'deceitful above all things and beyond cure. Who can understand it?' (Jeremiah 17:9). Only in Christ is it made new.

One final comment. Despite all the efforts of godless men, Christ, at the appointed time and according to his word, rose from the dead. After his resurrection he gave 'many convincing proofs that he was alive' (Acts 1:3), before being taken up into heaven, where he sat down at the right hand of God. Today as we look back to that day at the centre of history, when the Lamb of God bore the sins of the world and poured out his life-blood, the cross still stands tall on Calvary in the minds of believers, pointing ever heavenwards and reminding us of another day that is fast approaching. It is a day of consummate triumph, when Christ shall descend from his glory, not to be sacrificed a second time, but to bring salvation to those who are waiting for him, whom the Father chose in his Son before the creation of the world. On that day he will come down with the sound of victory reverberating through the heavens and the earth, with the trumpet call of God, and we shall all be changed — in a flash, in the twinkling of an eye, to be like him. And we shall sing a new song, " 'Where, O death, is your victory? Where, O death, is your sting?" The sting of death is sin, and the power of sin is the law. But thanks be to God! He gives us the victory through our Lord Jesus Christ' (1 Corinthians 15:55-57). What joy shall fill our hearts, what peace transcending all human understanding shall reign, what perfect love will be ours, and all because the Lord of glory was crucified!